THE

G

THE LAST BASTION OF RACISM?
Gypsies, Travellers and policing

John Coxhead

Trentham Books
Stoke on Trent, UK and Sterling, USA

Trentham Books
Westview House   22883 Quicksilver Drive
734 London Road   Sterling
Oakhill   VA 20166-2012
Stoke on Trent   USA
Staffordshire
England St4 5NP

© 2007 John Coxhead

First published 2007

British Catalogue-in- Publication Data
A catalogue for this book is available from the British Library

ISBN: 1 85856 390 9

Front cover illustration copyright *Pride not Prejudice*

Designed and typeset by Trentham Print design Ltd, Chester and printed in Great Britain by Hobbs the Printers Ltd, Hampshire.

No one is born hating another person because of the colour of his skin, or his background, or his religion. People must learn to hate.

Nelson Mandela, *Long Walk to Freedom* (2004: 749)

Contents

Acknowledgements

Whilst this book has been many years in the making, informed by practice and experience, its content is based mainly on doctoral research. The research was only possible because of the contributions of the Romany and Roma Gypsy and Irish Traveller communities, and other professionals in the public services, in the UK, Europe and North America. I have spent a good proportion of my life working with Gypsies and Travellers, and their voices have shaped my insights which, in turn, I will share with you.

There are many people I need to thank for keeping me to the point, particularly Siobhan and DGLG, Peter, Patrick, Gyorgy, Marie, John and Gillian. My family has tiptoed around the tapping of the keyboard; Michelle has longed for it all to be finished and Katie and Olivia perhaps wonder what exactly I have been doing. Hopefully all will become clearer as they grow older.

P.G. Wodehouse expressed it well when he suggested writers simply apologise for what they write, rather than give lengthy explanations. I perhaps have perhaps bitten off more than I can chew in writing a book on the 'last bastion of racism'. Further, I dread letting down the tragic but powerful legacy left by Johnny and Patrick Delaney. This worries me because the subject matter is important and urgent.

Taking the valuable contributions given to me through the communities and delivering them to the public at large gives me a heavy responsibility. I hope I can reach a wide readership since the issues in this book are specifically about Gypsies and Travellers but are also more widely concerned with the human condition of bigotry. I hope there are generic insights for many to apply, and I thank Simon Leckie for supporting this outlook in his valuable contribution in Chapter One.

I hope I have done enough to make the points that need making, to make people think, and to inform the development of professional practice in tackling bigotry. Where I fail, the errors are mine alone.

John Coxhead
Nottinghamshire, 2007

Foreword
The legacy of Johnny Delaney

My 15 year old son, Johnny Delaney, was murdered in 2003, because he was a Traveller. I and my family were devastated by what happened, but we have vowed to help overcome the hatred that exists in society towards Gypsies and Travellers. The way forward is in bringing people together to develop mutual understanding and respect.

It is by working together that future generations can learn to live alongside each other. The legacy of Johnny Delaney is to overcome the prejudice and hatred that he met. Every step that takes us nearer to understanding each other and why hatred can become so destructive is a good step. This book is one of those steps.

I want to remind everyone that the problems we need to overcome are stubborn ones. But together, we can change things. That is the legacy of Johnny Delaney.

Patrick Delaney

I have worked all over Europe over the last forty years helping promote improved relations between Gypsies, Travellers and policing and Justice Workers. During this time I have been President of the Gypsy Council, a member of the International Romani Union Parliament and now Chair of The National Federation of Gypsy Groups, made up of a network of community members.

It strikes me that the problems we face are due to a lack of mutual understanding. Based on my experience and desire to see improvement, I welcome *The Last Bastion of Racism*. I will tell you why.

The book is based on research carried out with Gypsies and Travellers. It has been able to capture the key issues facing communities, and involved them in problem solving and finding solutions. That makes it quite unique.

This book may be based on complicated analysis, but the suggestions are practical. I commend *The Last Bastion of Racism* to everyone to reconsider the inclusion of Travellers and Gypsies but also to help overcome all racism, everywhere.

My final words must go to the legacy of the Irish Traveller Johnny Delaney. Johnny was 15 years old when he was murdered. Since then his father Patrick campaigned for justice and a better future where bigotry will be a thing of the past. Patrick died in 2005, leaving us, yes, with the tragedy of Johnny's murder, but also with a legacy to make change. Remember Johnny Delaney, and remember why we all need to fight racism.

Peter Mercer MBE

1

Introduction

This is a positive book about a challenging subject. My purpose is to help inform a brighter future despite evidence of a gloomy past. So even though there is a warts and all exposé of the issues, the purpose remains to look forward. The book presents, and builds upon, the data and findings of research involving justice sector professionals and representatives from the Irish Traveller and Romany Gypsy communities. The research focus was a problem solving exploration of attitudes towards Gypsies and Travellers, to inform improving professional policing practice. The data was collected between May 2003 and February 2005.

A wealth of qualitative data provided deep insight into the long-term problem of the relationship between the communities and policing provision in the UK. The active contributions from justice practitioners and strategists all working together alongside Travellers and Gypsies, all working together to improve mutual understanding created a whole series of dynamic insights. During analysis, the data was shared and discussed with a Reference Group, which included Eastern European representatives to incorporate the pan European context of Roma (Coxhead, 2005; Zsaru, 2005).

The policing relationship with Romany Gypsies and Irish Travellers has been poor for several decades, evidenced by a mutual lack of trust, respect and co-operation. Police training has often omitted issues facing Travellers. Where Traveller issues have been raised, many police trainers identify cases of overt racism from police audiences, which trainers are unable to address effectively.

Despite much race and diversity development in policing as a whole, contemporary attitudes towards Travellers still reveal overt racism. An initial focus on the police training environment reveals wider symptoms in the policing workplace, which in turn highlights the need for institutional level change.

Diversity training in the police service has become particularly specialised, thus creating a cultural ethos where diversity issues are sometimes seen as HQ business, and not relevant to street policing. The cultural gulf between training and police operations weakens any strategies to purely 'out train' racism and prejudice. This points to the need to focus on behaviours in workplace core performance to change working culture. To focus on the workplace a new skills shift is required to move police trainers' traditional techniques to more everyday use by workplace supervisors. Workplace supervisors become the new trainers or more accurately, performance coaches. Such development removes traditional barriers and limitations of the classroom, whilst retaining the best techniques in developing people's skills in race and diversity performance.

This research brings together community representation, police trainers, and policing advisors in a problem solving approach to analyse the current situation, and develop practical improvements to change professional practice in police training and operations. The findings illustrate the importance of leadership, and extensive community engagement, as crucial to improving performance in race and diversity. Combined with leadership, the need to focus on workplace development means much less reliance on training as a single solution.

Aims of the research

The purpose of the research was to improve practice in service delivery for Gypsies and Travellers. This was specifically in the context of policing performance, but would apply to the justice sector as a whole. Further, the issues are so broad there is direct relevance for public sector workers in general, who have duties under the Race Relations (Amendment) Act, 2000.

The research initially explored training methods approaches, but emergent findings broadened out the inquiry towards a much wider examination of organisational and cultural level influences beyond just training. There is, nevertheless, a good amount of research data and findings examining specific issues in learning and development, which will be of interest to educationalists, trainers and those working in race equality. For example, there is a focus on the uses of educational psychology (Wolfendale, *et al*, 1991) for learning strategies which also draws on previous research on behaviourism.

A final and perhaps overriding purpose in the research was the ethical and moral purpose in seeking the authentic highlighting of an unacceptable situation facing Romany Gypsies and Irish Travellers. I had been in close contact with the Delaney family, working with Patrick, and hearing first hand from the family of the devastating effects of the murder of Johnny Delaney. Patrick, who died during the time of the research, made it clear that whilst Johnny's death was tragic, it was also a legacy. This legacy was a restless and positive conscience reminding that such tragedy must not be allowed to happen again – something must be done. In this sense, this book is the culmination of my efforts to put the agenda on the table for both specialists and the general public: the rest needs more than me to make lasting change.

Methodology and research design

The research method was selected to support an action research (Hill and Kerber, 1967) and problem solving approach (Eck and Spelman, 1988). The use of focus groups facilitated deep meanings beyond survey techniques (Cacciapuoti, 1998), by utilising practitioner insight (Holdaway, 1996). After extensive piloting, two substantive focus groups were set up involving practitioners and the community, in-groups of nine to fourteen people (Goss and Leinbach, 1996). The focus group membership reflected a national spread, with no focus on any one geographical area. The data was discussed and analysed using the whole cohort of focus group attendees in a web based forum, for respondent validation (McCormick and James, 1983; Lather, 1991).

The author's contribution to the research setting

I was well known amongst the community and with policing and justice professionals for my views that more needed to be done to tackle racism. This is exactly the sort of issue that inevitably prompts concerns over validity, respondent bias and the Hawthorne effect in research (Belson, 1986). Strenuous efforts were taken to ensure informed consent, open access, inclusivity, anonymity, and a facilitative (not contributory) role as researcher (Zeni, 1998; Macklin, 1999).

A reference group comprising those contributing to the focus groups oversaw the analysis of data through to the saturation of conclusions and findings through continued interaction (Kitzinger, 1994). Making sense with others was key in balancing any potential bias, by ensuring minimum researcher moderation (Krueger, 1993). This independent voice from delegates can be evidenced in the research focus moving from one of training to wider service delivery. Such a move demonstrates the drive of authentic emergent findings rather than any 'contamination' (Scriven, 1986) by the researcher's inherent perceptions.

Bias and representation in the research

The methodology of seeking 'emergence' and 'saturation' (Glaser, 1992) of key issues was to counter any researcher predisposition and bias. The situational ethno-methodological (Garfinkel, 1968; Burrel and Morgan, 1979) approach helped address the problem of power imbalance in research (Bernstein, 1974), meaning in simple terms the data was both provided and analysed by practitioners and community. The emphasis was placed upon participant 'voice' and 'democratisation' (Van de Ven and Delbecq, 1974), with the researcher acting as a low-key facilitator.

Ethical considerations

Establishing informed consent (Jupp, 1989) was paramount for the research, within the particular pressures of focus groups (Gibbs, 1997). Establishing a non threatening environment (Morgan, 1993) and the protection of anonymity (Powney and Watts, 1987) were vital to research confidence and trust. From the outset, given the highly charged nature of the subject matter, it was emphasised that these ethical safeguards would apply beyond the research into dissemination and publication (Zeni, 1998).

Data sample collection

The concerns of replicability, representativeness and reliability (Oppenheim, 1992) are important to ensure the authenticity and integrity of data in research. I identified two key informant groups. Firstly there were the representatives of Romany Gypsies and Irish Travellers, two distinct ethnic groups. Secondly, the professional practitioners: trainers, policing delivery, strategic workers and those who inspect and monitor the quality of policing.

Methods

Method is informed by purpose. My research context was informed by an early questionnaire used with policing trainers in 2003, with a return rate of 59 per cent. Here I found 100 per cent of respondents experienced racism towards Gypsies and Travellers, with 64 per cent feeling professionally inadequate in challenging this.

I developed a research aim to identify challenges for practitioners and develop practice, exploring possible solutions, by working with key partners, to achieve improved professional practice in the workplace.

I constructed four central research questions:

1. What were practitioners' experiences of prejudice towards Gypsies and Travellers?

2. Were there any patterns of such experiences, and why?

3. Did practitioners find this area challenging, and if so, why?

4. What insights were there (at analysis and solutions stages) in problem solving this?

Focus groups were a good way of utilising aspects of grounded theory (Glaser and Strauss, 1967; Glaser, 1992), enabling the dynamic interaction of mixed respondents to discuss a central problem. Open coding allowed emergence to guard against the researcher seeing what they might wish to see (Zeni, 1998), and further the whole process of research itself offered a positive intervention in the social world (Halsey, 1972).

I paid particular attention to a Socratic role as researcher (Carr and Kemmis, 1986) to learn from points that Winter (1989; 1998) makes about action research validation. Over controlling the process of data collection was also a concern, recognising the importance of 'mess' in research (Cook, 1998). The primary benefit of focus groups and open coding was to facilitate 'voice' and democracy (Stringer, 1999), hence the need for the researcher to avoid any temptation to control or overly interfere.

Analysis

The open coding approach (Babchuk, 1997) took into account both emic and etic perspectives. Coding was refined by the use of three stages outlined by Yoong, *et al*, (2004):

■ open conceptual coding and labelling of data

■ connections sought

■ comparison of data connections using emerging theory towards saturation

Reporting the findings

Whilst the research was supervised throughout by the Department of Education in the University of Derby, analysis and findings were also shared widely with the community. The data informed a Home Office publication called *Moving Forward* (2005) in partnership with DGLG, supported by a Queen's Award. The resultant recommendations from *Moving Forward* continue to be scrutinised, and utilised in the skills development focus of improving policing performance in race and diversity. The contemporary focus on workplace skills and leadership signals a move towards more recognition of the cultural and psychological nature of the problems of bigotry and racism.

The situation of Gypsies and Travellers is specific, but offers generic insights into combating other forms of racism and bigotry. To reinforce this point, I canvassed the national strategic lead for the Sector Skills Council for the Justice Sector (Skills for Justice) to write the first part of this book. The need to move beyond a training approach to make effective progress is the central finding from the research. This is a point well received by the Sector Skills Council, who realise the importance of workplace skills and behaviours.

Simon Leckie and Dick Winterton are to be congratulated for their ongoing national efforts to implement pragmatic skills development, to improve confidence and trust in the justice sector. Simon Leckie, for the remainder of this introductory chapter, explains why what follows in the rest of this book offers an effective skills-based approach for tackling bigotry of all kinds.

The skills we need to achieve justice for all
Simon Leckie

As the national lead for diversity and leadership in Skills for Justice, my role is to promote the National Occupational Standards as a way of ensuring a common minimum standard of behaviour in race and diversity for the justice sector in England and Wales.

With a history that you can trace to the 1970s, race and diversity training in the police service has probably undergone more scrutiny than any other type of training delivered. New approaches were introduced following the Scarman Report in 1981 and the Macpherson Report in 1999 and as a result of these and other reports, race and diversity training has been under continual development. The Home Office, the Association of Police Authorities, the Association of Chief Police Officers and Centrex have developed *A strategy for improving performance in race and diversity 2004-2009*. This strategy is being implemented through the Police Race and Diversity Learning and Development Programme (PRDLDP). It sets challenging goals for the police that will, if met, help the service to move forward.

Embedded within the PRDLDP are National Occupational Standards (NOS) for diversity. This puts a real focus on what people actually do, thereby placing core performance as the central issue; a move many people welcome. There is much good work being done and NOS provide a mechanism to show this. But what are the NOS? NOS describe competent performance in terms of the outcomes of an individual's work and define the knowledge and skills they need to perform effectively in the workplace. They allow a clear assessment of competence against nationally agreed standards of performance, across a range of workplace circumstances for all roles. In this way, defining what has to be achieved rather than just what an individual needs to know, they provide the flexibility required to meet the needs of individuals.

The Home Office report *Moving Forward* has identified the need for more emphasis on leadership to 'outperform prejudice'. The view is that it is logical to recognise the crucial role that ethical leadership has in driving performance in race and diversity and its leadership. Training will continue to play an important part in ensuring that people understand what respect for race and diversity means and why respect for race and diversity is a fundamental principle of day-to-day policing. But training alone is not enough and everyone in the police has to help create a culture in the service that will not tolerate a lack of respect for race and diversity.

The history of race and diversity for the police service has been all about trying to get the impact to service delivery. The approaches described in *The Last Bastion* show the way ahead for addressing diversity and put the emphasis where it needs to be – in the workplace. In the future, leadership will increasingly drive diversity as core business, and we'll start referring to race and diversity as 'what we do'.

A new perspective

Some companies and public sector organisations resort to mandatory diversity training courses for everyone. However, this decision credits training with powers it doesn't possess. The root of the problem lies in the company's culture and its management policies and practices. William Tate: *Leadership in organisations – current issues and key trends*

Attempts at addressing diversity have tended to focus on the knowledge aspect of learning and development. Training courses have dealt largely in theory and discussed diversity in the workplace from a hypothetical, somewhat artificial perspective. Whilst the earlier programmes have undoubtedly helped raise awareness in relation to diversity, they have done little to challenge people's actual behaviour in the workplace. Much of the criticism levelled at these earlier programmes is related to the lack of relevance of what was taught to people's day to day operational roles. Diversity was often discussed in abstract terms, inadvertently positioning it as something additional to normal duties. The language used was often academic and complex, making diversity seem difficult to understand let alone apply to an operational policing context. This was obviously not the intended outcome and the police's experience of diversity is no different to many others. Early attempts at addressing diversity in many sectors are characterised by a focus on theory and the resultant disconnection between operational practitioners and diversity.

By focusing on diversity in isolation and seeing the key learning outcome as imparting knowledge about diversity, earlier programmes missed a critical point – that valuing diversity should be seen as a key value for the organisation and be embedded within organisational culture.

There are numerous theories (Handy, 1993; Schein, 2004) relating to organisational culture, some of which argue that it cannot be categorised or influenced by the organisation (Smirchich, 1983). However, if you accept – as I do – that it can be influenced then it's clear that leaders have a key role in promoting the values and beliefs that will enable the desired culture to flourish. Seen in this way addressing the behaviour and performance of leaders must be a key component of any attempt to address diversity in the workplace and the PRDLDP states that 'an organisational culture must be created which leads to operational policing taking on a strong ethical dimension'.

Ethical leadership
The ethical dimension of leadership features strongly in many leadership theories (Covey, 1999) and is reflected in the recently developed[1] Police Leadership Qualities Framework (PLQF) which includes Personal Integrity as one of its three key principles.

Principle-centred leadership
In his book *Principle-Centred Leadership* Covey gives some examples of leadership dilemmas that cannot be resolved by using conventional approaches:

- How do I balance personal and professional areas of life in the middle of constant crises and pressures?

- How can I be genuinely happy for the successes and competencies of another?

- How do we maintain control, yet give people the freedom and autonomy they need to be effective in their work?

You may recognise some of these dilemmas yourself. Covey argues that they cannot be solved by common approaches to leadership. He believes that we are all subject to natural laws or governing principles. The natural laws are based on principles and operate regardless of our awareness of or obedience to them. Covey points out that, 'the only thing that endures over time is the law of the farm: I must prepare the ground, put in the seed, cultivate it, weed it, water it, then gradually nurture growth and development to full maturity'. There is no quick fix in leading and developing yourself and your people; what endures over time are principles. Covey stresses that principles need to be at the centre of your life, the centre of your relationships, the centre of your management contracts, the centre of the entire organisation.

According to Covey, correct principles are like a compass – they will always point the way. What's vital is that you know how to read them so you don't get lost, confused, or fooled by conflicting voices and values. Principles apply at all times in all places and surface in the form of values, ideas, norms and teachings that uplift, ennoble, fulfill, empower and inspire people.

Covey sets out a four-level model:

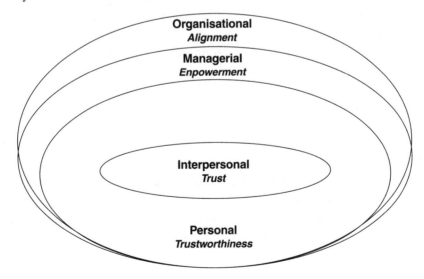

Covey stresses that principle-centred leadership is practiced from the inside out on four levels:

- *Personal* – my relationship with myself

- *Interpersonal* – my relationships and interactions with others

- *Managerial* – my responsibility to get a job done with others

- *Organisational* – my need to organise people, to recruit them, train them, compensate them, build teams, solve problems and create aligned structure, strategy and systems.

It's worth reflecting on what this means, in particular the first two principles because of the role they play in your leadership and how you influence those around you.

Trustworthiness is based on character: what you are as a person and what you can do. Remember this later when we consider the National Occupational Standards and your competence. Covey argues that without character and competence we won't be considered trustworthy by others, neither will we show much wisdom in our choices and decisions.

If trustworthiness is the foundation of trust then trust is the emotional bank account between two people that enables them to have a win-win performance agreement. In Covey's view, if two people trust each other, based on the trustworthiness of each other, they can enjoy effective communication, empathy, synergy and productive interdependency.

If you accept Covey's arguments, you will see that respecting and valuing diversity is not going to be achieved merely by reading a book or undertaking e-learning or attending a training session. These quick fixes may help increase your knowledge and understanding but they are just a small part of what's needed. People need a clear understanding of their own values and beliefs and any prejudices they have, and then gain a sense of what principles they truly believe in – what inviolate truths provide them with guiding principles.

The Police Leadership Qualities Framework

In 2004 a Home Office report into police leadership *Police leadership: Expectations and Impact* identified that between a quarter and a third of line managers within the Police Service were not having a positive impact upon their staff. This report also identified that there was no clear model for leadership within the Police Service.

The Home Office report recommended that key stakeholders, in particular the Police Leadership Development Board, Skills for Justice and the National Police Leadership Centre at Centrex (now renamed the Leadership Academy for Policing) should begin to develop an evidence-based model, detailing the key elements of effective police leadership.

In October 2004 the Police Leadership Development Board initiated research by the Leadership Academy for Policing at Centrex to identify the key qualities required for police leadership.

The Police Leadership Qualities Framework (PLQF) is the product of that research and sets out the key qualities required for police leadership. These key qualities underpin the behavioural competencies shown in the Integrated Competency Framework (ICF) behavioural framework. The three key qualities are:

- personal integrity
- personal awareness
- passion for achievement

The ICF behavioural framework describes the key behavioural competencies that are important for effective performance across all roles in the Police Service. Because they are strongly based on behaviour, the ICF competencies are clustered in ways that relate closely to the tasks being undertaken – for example effective communication, problem solving, and planning and organising.

By contrast, the PLQF describes the key qualities required for effective leadership within the Police Service. The PLQF qualities underlie the ICF behavioural competences and are based primarily on inner attributes such as values, beliefs and attitudes. Because of this, they are more difficult to observe, and tend to show themselves to one extent or another through all of the ICF behavioural competencies.

The PLQF consists of 69 items clustered under the three headings of Personal Integrity, Personal Awareness, and Passion for Achievement.

The relationship between the ICF behavioural competencies and the PLQF qualities is shown graphically below. Because the three PLQF qualities tend to show themselves to one extent or another through all of the ICF behavioural competencies, they form a core of values, beliefs and attitudes that underpin the twelve ICF behavioural competencies.

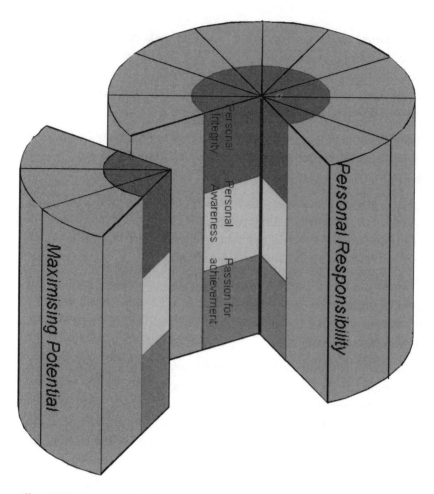

All 69 PLQF items relate directly to one of the ICF Behavioural Competencies.

Covey's Principle-Centred Leadership and the PLQF emphasise the importance to effective leadership of qualities and values. If organisations have leaders who believe in and value diversity and display these beliefs in the leadership of their people, diversity will no longer be seen as difficult to understand or unrelated to 'real world' activity. It is therefore vital that diversity is positioned and addressed as a leadership issue, not as a discrete topic.

The $64m question

Whilst few people would argue that leadership has a key role to play in creating an organisational culture that values diversity, the actual development of the leadership skills needed to help bring this to reality can be somewhat problematic. This is largely because whilst we all accept terms like integrity we each have differing ideas about what integrity actually means.

There are numerous leadership models and theories, many of which include integrity as a key feature of effective leadership but what you won't find is one definition of integrity. This can pose real difficulties when trying to determine the current capability of leaders – just what are we measuring our leaders against? Another difficulty arises from the fact that it is incredibly hard to determine what people's beliefs and values really are. By their very nature, beliefs and values are deeply rooted in each person's psyche and operate at a subconscious level. The following diagram shows how values and beliefs sit near the centre of the range of human attributes.

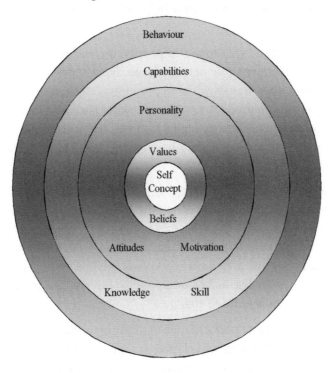

This model can be likened to the layers of an onion with a person's behaviour being the first thing that is usually noticed. In this model the different levels are influenced from the centre out so that values and beliefs affect personality, attitudes and motivation, and this in turn influences the capabilities, knowledge and skill which ultimately affect how someone behaves. Whilst no-one can determine what anybody else truly values and believes in, anybody can see how somebody else behaves and from this can draw some conclusions about what they believe.

You may be thinking 'but what does this have to do with ethical leadership?' which leads nicely into the use of NOS! At the start of this section I outlined how difficult it can be to be to define what you're looking for from leaders, particularly when exploring the less tangible aspects of exemplary leadership like integrity. The next section shows how NOS can help define what leaders need to do in order to display the behaviours required for a culture that values diversity to flourish.

Defining exemplary leadership

We have looked at Covey's Principle-Centred Leadership model and how competence is a critical element of trustworthiness. This is where the use of NOS can have real impact and really help define what leaders need to do to promote diversity.

Note first that NOS are developed to provide a clear definition about what competence in any given role actually looks like. Competence is a standardised requirement for an individual to properly perform a specific job. It encompasses a combination of knowledge, skills and behaviour utilised to improve performance. More generally, competence is the state or quality of being adequately or well qualified, having the ability to perform a specific role.

For instance, management competency includes the traits of systems thinking and emotional intelligence and skills in influence and negotiation. A person possesses a competence as long as the skills, abilities and knowledge that constitute that competence are a part of them, enabling them to perform effective action within a certain workplace environment. Therefore, one might not lose knowledge, a skill, or an ability, but still lose a competence if what is needed to do a job well changes.

NOS describe competent performance in terms of outcomes. Together with a defined assessment strategy, developed in parallel with the standards, they allow a clear assessment of competence against nationally agreed standards of performance, across a range of workplace circumstances for all roles.

Today, NOS are viewed by modern managers as an indispensable tool for managing a highly skilled workforce. They are used widely to support individual and organisational development and quality assurance at all levels. They provide benchmarks of good practice across the UK.

National Occupational Standards form the basis of qualifications, most commonly National Vocational Qualifications (NVQs) and Scottish Vocational Qualifications (SVQs). They define individual competence in performance terms – the successful outcome of work activity. They are concerned with what people can do, not just what they know. They promote industry best practice, and have been developed by operational practitioners covering all parts of the justice sector.

Occupational Standards have great value and utility within all sectors. They can, for example, be used for recruitment and selection, job design and evaluation, training needs analysis, learning programmes and performance appraisals. Good employers invest in training their staff in order to remain competitive; at the same time this provides individuals with improved skills and opportunities for career development. The standards provide an essential benchmark for all this activity.

Working with people from across the justice sector, Skills for Justice has developed a NOS titled 'Promote equality and value diversity' The summary for this NOS describes it as follows:

> This unit is about promoting equality and valuing the diversity of people. This is an essential aspect of all jobs in the justice sector and is appropriate to people working at all levels and in all posts. It should form the basis of everything that any worker in the sector does.[2]

This NOS defines the performance criteria required to demonstrate competence with a particular focus on what people actually do and includes criteria such as:

■ act in ways that

  ☐ acknowledge and recognise individuals' background and beliefs

  ☐ respect diversity

  ☐ value people as individuals

  ☐ do not discriminate against people

■ take account of how your behaviour affects individuals and their experience of your organisation's culture and approach

■ seek feedback from individuals on your behaviour and use this to improve what you do in the future

This unit also defines what people need to know and understand, one of which relates directly to organisational culture: 'how your behaviour contributes to your organisation's culture and your responsibility for creating a positive culture for all'.

The NOS for promoting diversity provides a clear, consistent measure of what good performance in diversity actually looks like and so removes much of the ambiguity surrounding what leaders actually need to do in order to create a culture within their organisation that values diversity.

Enhancing leadership skills

Skills Foresight research undertaken by Skills for Justice and the current Sector Skills Agreement process have identified management and leadership skills as a key area for development across the breadth of the Justice sector. The mapping of current management and leadership development activity in Northern Ireland and Scotland shows that a wide range of programmes are currently in use. However, this remains a key issue and the majority of current programmes employ traditional methods of skills development through formal teaching to distance and e-learning.

Action learning provides a different approach, where participants, guided by facilitators, learn from each other and then apply the learning in the work-place to tackle a real business issue. The learning thus takes place throughout the duration of the action learning programme and is not confined to the classroom. Action learning has the additional benefits of providing a structured way of stimulating cross-organisational learning and the develop-ment of self-sustaining groups that can last long after the actual programme has been completed. The Last Bastion provides compelling evidence that action learning principles are extremely useful in working with communities to address problems and build relationships.

There is a clear need to consider new approaches to management and leader-ship development within the justice sector. There is also a need, and a willing-ness, to open up learning across organisational boundaries and action learn-ing could be used to support multi-agency learning and address some of the challenges facing the Justice sector.

Action learning could be used to build on the management and leadership development programmes currently in use by providing an opportunity for experienced managers to apply their learning and share experiences to resolve real problems that are blocking improvements in their organisation's performance.

Action learning can

■ address real problems being experienced in the workplace

■ enable people from different agencies to support one another by sharing knowledge and experiences

■ build on existing management and leadership development activities

16

■ become self-sustaining, enabling employers to run action learning programmes as and when they wish

■ be delivered at low cost

■ help to build informal support networks across the sector

There is some confusion about what action learning actually is. The phrase 'action learning' has become one of the current management buzzwords and is used, often incorrectly, to describe a wide range of management development activities. The following definitions, taken from the International Foundation for Action Learning http://www.ifal.org.uk, apply whenever the term to action learning as used in this report:

■ A powerful form of problem solving combined with intentional learning in order to bring about change in individuals and the organisation.

■ Essential elements of action learning are

  – tackling real tasks in the real world and the real role

  – learning with and through each other

  – taking individual responsibility and actually implementing solutions and plans.

■ At the heart of the process is the 'action learning set' – a group who meet at regular intervals for each member to explore a challenging open-ended problem or opportunity. Every member works on their 'task' and the others, as friends, provide support and challenge. The aim is to help each member both to tackle the task and to learn from doing so.

■ A basic premise of action learning is that: 'there is no learning without action and no (sober and deliberate) action without learning' (Reg Revans)

■ By using the knowledge and experience of a small group of people combined with skilled questioning, individuals are enabled to re-interpret old and familiar concepts and produce fresh ideas – often without needing new knowledge.

From these definitions the key features of action learning include learning through sharing the knowledge and experience of a small group to address real world problems, often supported by formal training inputs. A current feature of action learning is that the process is usually supported by a facilitator who guides and supports the action learning set.

The features of action learning[3] are compared in this table with traditional approaches to management and leadership development:

Action learning	Existing approaches
Action on real tasks or problems at work	Learning **not directly linked** to real tasks or problems and difficult to establish link between programme and individual's jobs/role
Learning is from **reflections** on action taken	Learning is from trainer/course material
Tasks/problems are **individual** rather than collective	Typically designed to deliver **collective** learning experience, usually on a generic management and leadership theme
Tasks/problems are chosen **independently** by individuals	Aims and objectives set for the **group**
Questioning as the main way to help participants proceed with their problems	**Telling** as the main way to help participants proceed with their problems
Facilitators are used	**Trainers** are used

The benefits of action learning

Action learning is significantly different to many of the existing approaches used for management and leadership development across the sector. People who took part in the SSDA action learning pilot made the following comments:

'I have benefited greatly from this programme and have been able to bring the benefits directly back to my business'

'The programme has really helped me to gain the confidence and achieve changes'

'This has contributed to us now achieving a bid success rate of one out of two, when previously we only succeeded in one out of seven bids'

'This programme has helped me to reflect on my position and consider my options for the future'

'This has already helped to increase my new orders by fifty per cent and there is a feeling that all the staff are more motivate'.

'I have significantly improved relationships with the staff, who will now approach me with problems, rather than hiding them from me. In this way, we have been able to look for a solution, rather than allocate blame. We are already seeing improved profitability, due to less quality problems.'

'My business partner is now committed and on board to help me make strategic changes. This has been a major achievement'

Participants also reported the following key business benefits and leadership skills development:

Key business benefits	Leadership skills development
■ Culture change in their business	■ Enhanced confidence
■ Reduced wastage and improved production	■ Improved delegation
■ Staff restructuring	■ Promoting and managing change
■ Improvement in staff morale and motivation	■ Negotiating
	■ Communicating with the business
	■ Balancing work/life priorities

As can be seen from these examples, action learning can deliver real impact to both the individuals on the programme and the organisation that they work in. For the Justice sector the benefits of action learning include:

■ Building on existing management and leadership programmes by providing a structured programme in which knowledge and skills can be applied to real world problems

■ Solving existing organisational problems that appear to have no obvious solution, for example:

☐ working in a multi-agency partnership where organisational cultures and priorities conflict

☐ delivering the modernisation agenda with fixed, or even reduced, resources

☐ integrating performance appraisal with operational activity to create a performance coaching culture

☐ sense of unease and firm belief that things should be better – where the exact nature of what is 'wrong' is not clear

☐ Sharing knowledge and experience across the sector

■ Building supportive networks across the sector, characterised by trust, openness, honesty and respect that have a proven track record of being able to help

■ Greater awareness of other organisations by taking a wider perspective and being able to see common problems from a different perspective

■ Development of individuals and the organisation they work in

Conclusion

If the justice sector is to meet the needs and expectations of all members of the community then a genuine respect for, and valuing of, diversity has to become embedded within the organisational cultures of the organisations in which we work.

We need to be absolutely clear on two points:

■ training courses will not achieve this on their own.

■ diversity should be addressed as part of leadership development, not as a stand-alone subject

This is because leadership is a key factor in shaping organisational culture. It's what leaders consistently say and do that shapes the way people view 'the way we do things around here' so it influences everyone's behaviour.

Previous approaches to addressing diversity failed to deliver the intended outcomes because they tended to concentrate on diversity from a theoretical, often abstract perspective. Whilst these programmes helped to improve people's knowledge and understanding regarding diversity they failed to help translate this into changes in their behaviour and improvements in their skills at dealing with others.

One definition of insanity is: persistently repeating the same thing but expecting to get a different result. It's time for a new look at diversity and for taking a different approach – one that focuses on developing skills and helps people get a clear idea about what they need to do. This book gives us just such a springboard to revitalise and advance professional practice. It uses a case study approach to create innovative strategies such as 'outperforming prejudice', 'inside out' and 'exploding skills' to empower workplace leadership. I commend *The Last Bastion of Racism?* to you as an essential, practical guide to delivering real improvements in how we interact with all members of the communities we serve.

Notes

1 The PLQF has been included with the Integrated Competency Framework behavioural frame-work, thereby ensuring it will be used across all police human resource processes.

2 To view this in full go to http://www.skillsforjustice.com/websitefiles/NOS_COMMON_AA1(1). pdf

3 What has action learning learned to become?, Mike Pedler, John Burgoyne and Cheryl Brook

2

Setting the scene

This book is aimed at practitioners and policy makers who are working in a practical way to overcome bigotry, prejudice and racism. One of my main motivations for writing it is to make a different contribution to many existing volumes which seem to me to obfuscate the issues by discussing bigotry as an ethereal or theoretical debate. Let me be clear on my views: firstly, bigotry ruins people's lives. Usually, it is *someone else's* life. Secondly, bigotry is essentially the problem of the person carrying the bigotry, who transfers this problem to affect others. Thirdly, bigotry may be an old and apparently irreconcilable phenomenon, but I believe it *can be* overcome. Fourthly, I believe it is a necessity for the future advancement of humanity that bigotry is overcome.

I have been able to prepare this book for general use after carrying out extensive research about the racism facing Romany Gypsies and Irish Travellers. Whilst the specific issues facing Gypsies and Travellers are just that – specific – the research also offers *generic* lessons about all prejudice. It has struck me time and again that the issues arising out of my applied research are generically applicable.

In discussing racism the point I wish to emphasise about generic principles means I do not wish us to be drawn into such discussions as I have sadly experienced which appear to be an ironic competition about where the greatest 'ism' lies. What I can tell you is that in my research I consciously went to the examples I could find of the most overt and most extreme forms of bigotry and prejudice, and these turned out to be towards Gypsies and Travellers. If these extreme issues can be tackled, there are lessons for everyone. As for this being the last bastion of racism? Well, I'll come back to that.

In setting the scene, let me explain that the research to inform this book has taken a *problem solving* approach to seek out practical ways of making improvement in policing, across the justice sector and wider afield for public services as a whole. From the outset it was quite clear that there was a problem to be addressed, and one that had a long history marred by poor relations of distrust: 'over policing and under protecting'. In problem solving the nature of the symptoms one must be clear about *who* the focus is. Throughout, my focus is in changing the bigot, not the bigot's target. The findings of this research come from the experience of people who have suffered racism. But the findings target perpetrators, not victims.

Importantly, this book, whilst focusing on the specific case study of Gypsies and Travellers, offers new generic lessons for tackling bigotry in every form. When I began the research that has led to the book you are reading, the focus was on finding ways of improving training practice. It is fair to say that the scope of the work enlarged, covering a wide series of issues beyond training, and involving an international perspective, particularly in Eastern Europe, as it went on. The wider the eventual influence the book has in tackling all bigotry – everywhere – the more worthwhile this research will have been.

The social historical context

Romany Gypsies and Irish Travellers have different social histories, and different identities. It is quite misleading to categorise 'Gypsy/Traveller' as one single entity, as is sometimes done in the popular media. The informed reader should appreciate the dangers of oversimplified labelling that lumps different groups as one. There are, however, commonalities between the two ethnic groups, and the experience of racism is a shared one. Since the purpose of this book is tackling bigotry, the groups are linked because the bigot does not differentiate when targeting them. Consequently, throughout this text the titles 'Gypsy' and 'Traveller' are used interchangeably when talking about their common experience of racism.

Romany Gypsies are believed to have moved from Northern India westwards, attracting the title Gypsies from a mistaken association to Little Egypt. The symbol adopted at the World Romani Congress in 1971 is a sixteen-spoked wheel, a link to the Roma's Indian origins (the 24-spoked *Ashok Chakra* is in the centre of the national flag of India, the *Tiranga*). Irish Travellers are a distinct group with their own language, and should not be confused with Romany Gypsies. Irish Travellers moved in substantial numbers to England in two distinct phases. The first followed the pressures of the potato famines in the 1800s and the growth of railway labour in the 1850s, and the second follow changes to Ireland's housing policy after 1963 (O'Hanlon, *et al*, 2004).

New Age Travellers are a diverse group. Case law has explored the more precise definitions of Gypsy and Traveller identity compared with New Age Travellers (Regina v. South Hams District Council and Another *ex parte*. Gibb; Leggatt J. in Berkshire County Council v. Bird [unreported], 26 September 1986). New Age Travellers do not have a defined ethnic status, and it is important to not confuse groups despite sometimes imprecise descriptions being used in the media (Lowe and Shaw, 1994; Kenrick and Clark 1999). O'Hanlon, *et al* (2004) provides a useful discussion of such distinctions that should be respected, including Showmen and Fairground communities.

Roma, or Rom, or in certain countries, Sinti, are believed to share the common root of Gypsy heritage, moving across Europe, and with a contemporary population of around 12 million. Records of Gypsies in England tend to be punitive and can be dated to the fifteenth century. In England, an Act was passed in 1530 which imposed a ban on 'Egipcions' entering the country and asked for those who were here to leave (Kenrick and Clark, 1999). By 1562 it was a hanging offence to be a Gypsy or to associate with one. Ivatts (2003) identifies that by the sixteenth century there was a consistent anti-Gypsy social climate right across Europe, with legal penalties often simply triggered by their existence. 'Gypsy hunts' were common in Germany between 1416 and 1774, complete with severed heads as trophies of the sport. Simply being a Gypsy was often illegal, or represented fair game for socially acceptable attack. In 1899, in Munich, The Central Office for Fighting the Gypsy Nuisance was established. In 1909, in Hungary, the suggestion was that all Gypsies should be branded for easy identification. By 1912, in France, all Gypsies over the age of six were forced to carry identity cards. In 1922, in Germany, social gatherings of Gypsies were banned. The Holocaust in the 1940s was the extreme example of genocidal intent (Friedman, 1990).

The Gypsy Holocaust is known as the *Porrajmos* (the 'Great Devouring'). Some of the recognition of the plight of Gypsies in the Holocaust was late coming, as Bedford (1999) observes. Whilst there was a focus on reparation for the Jews, Gypsies were omitted and unrecognised. This despite suffering perhaps the biggest proportionate loss of any one race during the Nazi led atrocities, with estimates of at least half a million deaths. The Racial Hygiene and Criminal Biology Research Unit, led by Robert Ritter, tracked suspected Gypsy ancestry and established sinister pseudo scientific tests to explore their 'sub-human nature'. The notion of a Final Solution for Gypsies as well as Jews, gays and Jehovah's Witnesses was very real, supported by serious planning and systematic executions in camps such as Birkenau.

It is known that 250 Gypsy children were used for testing the newly developed Zyclon cyanide gas to establish its suitability for widespread use in concentration camps after 1940. Such atrocities were not formally recognised until long after the war, and only then was it clear that 80 per cent of the Gypsy population had been affected (Wiesenthal, 1986, 1989) right across Europe.

Although there were several Gypsy and Traveller war heroes who fought for the British Army, the 1939-1945 war had less of an impact on Gypsies in England than in countries under Nazi occupation. Increasingly however, stopping places in England have become a problem, with fewer common land opportunities and the decline of some of the seasonal rural industries. The Caravans Sites Act of 1968, which tried to address site provision, was never fully implemented. Lord Avebury described this as 'unfinished business' (Morris and Clements, 1999a). The Act was repealed and replaced in 1994 by the Criminal Justice and Public Order Act. The Public Order Act focused on powers for removing trespassers, and there has been very little dialogue to balance this agenda and address site provision until quite recently (CRE, 2004a).

Arthur Ivatts (1975) draws a connection between the findings of the Plowden Report (1967) and secondary school experiences to identify a cycle of deprivation, stigma and poor support for young Gypsies and Travellers. The Swann Report (1985), Ofsted (1999) and later DfES (2003) continued to report the very same issues. Gypsies and Travellers remain the most at risk group in education in this country.

The contemporary social context of racism for Gypsies and Travellers

Hancock (2002:53) describes the phenomenon of anti-gypsyism which informs the next pages. This is the viewing of Gypsies as 'less than equals'; of social stigma and power imbalance, and to a great extent, a view socially institutionalised. This is a unique condition from which to begin describing a group of people. Discussing this particular minority group with students when training for diversity, I have found overt hatred I have not observed directed at any other racial group.

Phillips (2004:1) reported that Gypsies and Travellers face racism 'incomparably worse' than any other ethnic group in the UK. I found similar concerns in O'Nions (1995) and Hancock (1996). One example of social stigma, or 'anti-gypsyism' in the literature concerned denial of the existence or status of Gypsies and Travellers (Okely, 1983; Kenrick and Clark, 1999). Niner (2002) asserts that the title 'Gypsy' needs clearer definition. The distinction between traditional Travellers and Gypsies and New Age Travellers is important since it is by general perceptions and vague interpretations of definitions in legislation that traditions and rights can be eroded. Debo (1995) explores the threats and challenges to North American Indian culture and racial status, and a clear parallel can be found between the Native North American and the European Traveller in this context. It exists in both the threat to lifestyle, heritage and ethnic identity, for example illustrated by Bethrong (1963) concerning the Southern Cheyennes, and also in evidence of the institutionalised activities of control and containment (Foreman, 1932).

There is extensive documentation of the social difficulties that Gypsies and Travellers experience in legally defending their racial identity (see *inter alia* Okely, 1983). In courts Gypsies and Travellers have to prove their racial identity to justify recognition in planning applications. Such apparent debate over identity is curious, given the clear legislation based on the Mandla Criteria, which defines ethnicity, including Gypsies and Travellers (see *Mandla v Lee*, 1983). The central point is *why* there is still a debate about ethnic status. Morris (2000b) offers some insight in her discussion of the social invisibility of Gypsies, including issues of identity and status. Such 'invisibility' or non-recognition of a racial group might reflect a social power imbalance.

This situation is also unique because of two legal definitions of 'Gypsy', one in Race Relations legislation, and a quite different one in Planning Law. In the curricula of some training, where Gypsies are included, the planning law definition of their racial status is mistakenly used (Avon and Somerset Constabulary, 2004). Conflicting legal definitions of racial status are unparalleled in any ethnic group in Europe, and can be confusing and also misleading. In Planning Law, for example, a Gypsy stops being a 'Gypsy' when they stop travelling because they are ill. Despite the inclusion of Gypsies and Travellers within Race Relations criteria, there is a problem with consistent recognition of afforded rights. Such a lack of recognition for the communities, often when they are at their most vulnerable in seeking a place to live, leads to considerable tension (Morris, 2001).

In the existing literature which discusses Gypsy and Traveller identities there is perhaps more significance in what is *not* said or excluded, than in what is said. The omission of Gypsy and Traveller as races, or the denial shown by the reluctance to capitalise the proper nouns suggest a deliberate non recognition for an identity protected by legislation. The recommendations of the

Stephen Lawrence Inquiry (Macpherson 1999) and subsequent articles about the 'new campaign' about racism (e.g. *Police* magazine, March 1999), and the omission of Gypsies and Travellers in the 'new' campaign against racism reinforces the invisibility of this race. Maybe such omission unwittingly tolerates and colludes with 'antigypsism'. Recent stop search proposals (16+1) and the most recent National Census (see 2000a) omit Gypsies and Travellers as a race: Gypsies and Travellers, poignantly, are 'others'.

The Race Relations Act (1976), the *subsequent Race Relations (Amendment) Act* (2000), and the *Human Rights Act* (1998) refer to offences of discriminating (directly or indirectly) against someone on grounds of their colour, race, nationality or national or ethnic origins. The Amendment Act of 2000 includes a recommendation made in the Stephen Lawrence Inquiry that race relations legislation must apply to the police. This Act adds specific offences of racist violence and harassment outlawing racial discrimination in all public functions and places a positive duty on public authorities to actively promote race equality.

Whilst the existence and *legal* status of Gypsies and Travellers in England is clear, for some reason there is not always *social* recognition (Morris, 2000; CRE, 2004a). There are three interesting themes concerning Traveller identity. The first shows the *invisibility* stigma, a second which shows, ironically, an *over* highlighting of *negative issues* in the media, and thirdly a phenomenon of perceived stereotypical categories of romantic or criminogenic Gypsies and Travellers.

These themes are visible in police training classrooms and the data revealed such views as quite mainstream and acceptable: ultimately part of a contemporary social consciousness. The invisibility stigma which rejects the ethnic status of Travellers is perhaps an extension of *extermination* rather than mere social exclusion (Allport, 1979). Such an interpretation would coincide with writings about Gypsies and Travellers feeling their existence, their way of life, their heritage – their very *identity* – is being attacked by the state itself (Hancock, 1996). Perhaps the serious implications of hostile attitudes towards Gypsies lies in the reality of societal attitudes reflecting less *leitkultur* (defining culture) and being exposed for being more *volkisch* (ethnic nationalism). This could mean the powerful cultural pressure for social conformity might illustrate more sinister overtones and intolerance of difference rather than just a pride in association. Perhaps the perceived *difference* that Gypsies represent simply cannot be tolerated by some parts of society?

When the abnormal becomes normal

Essed (1991:10) explains that extreme discourse can become normalised for the dominant group, so that racism is not even recognised, 'let alone problematised – by the dominant group.' So not only are Gypsies and Travellers sometimes invisible, but there is also an apathetic *denial* of racism within the dominant group which prevents any progress. The diversity trainer may be able to recognise the symptoms of racism but given the normalised extent of anti-gypsyism, I could see why trainers were frustrated about what to do over the issues of overt prejudice towards Gypsies and Travellers. The trainer could, quite literally, be totally alone, both in the classroom *and* the social and political world in looking to challenge such prejudice (Pizani Williams, 1994; Power, 2004).

Assessing the extent or parameters of this extreme discourse is important so as not to underestimate the uniqueness of the situation concerning this group. Part of the problem the research addressed was that only general symptoms had previously been identified and not any underlying cause. The research journey proved to me that previous designers of public service practitioner development material had failed to grasp the difficulty of the problem.

The diverse literature identifying the unique nature of institutional discrimination against Gypsies and Travellers reveals a bleak contemporary picture. In education provision, a large number of Traveller children's need are not met (Dept of Education and Science, 1985:756; Acton and Dalphinis, 2000, Morris, 2001) and Gypsy and Traveller children remain the most at risk within the UK educational system. In health provision, Morris and Clements (1999), Morris (2001) and Van Cleemput (2004) presented evidence of the highest mortality rate in Europe for both children and adults, and the greatest problems in even accessing treatment by general medical practitioners. In housing provision, Niner (2002) identified that most local authorities had little to no accommodation policy for Gypsies and very few consulted with them.

Media representation also provided extreme examples of racism. Quotes to be found included reference to 'scum', and that 'Hitler was right' (Morris, 2000a: 215; *Birmingham Evening Mail* 29.06.93). There was a lack of criminological statistics concerning criminality or victimisation (Pizani Williams, 1994; Dawson, 2000), yet this lack of data did not seem to affect popular opinion. MacGreil (1996) and Kenny (1997) suggest that the representation of Gypsies and Travellers point to a clear lower caste or apartheid situation. This then, was a disturbing process of socially accepted and *uniquely* normalised propaganda that fuels the unconscious. UNESCO (1977) termed the situation 'institutionalised intolerance'. I wondered whether incitement to racial hatred was not more appropriate.

Perhaps the situation of Travellers and Gypsies and policing has been simply overlooked (O'Nions, 1995), perhaps it has been massively underestimated (Hancock, 2002), perhaps it has been deliberately omitted. A Roma leader from Eastern Europe explained to me that Gypsies were the 'Parriah' all over the Europe and beyond. He described legends of Biblical reference accounting for a race forever to live their lives as 'untouchables'. For whatever reasons, the situation has seen little positive improvement over decades.

The problem seems to be compounded by a *distance* between officials like the police and Gypsies and Travellers, and since there is nothing to break this depressing cycle, misnomer and myth are perpetuated (Pizani Williams, 1994; Power, 2004). A distance is felt on both sides, with young police officers having entrenched views and young Travellers likewise, sometimes based only on what they have heard not what they have experienced.

Since the history seems to have experienced a form of time warp, the prejudice towards these communities now offers itself as a fascinating insight into just how far antiracism strategies and diversity training has succeeded in the general promoting of respect for others' difference. Prejudice like this was last exposed in the 1950s and '60s before and during the black civil rights movement (Phillips, 2004).

Enough of speculation and curiosity: the situation described involves real people describing their contemporary stories of injustice. The purpose of this book is to bring to the fore for the general public the historical and contemporary reality, but also the importance and urgency, of this long overlooked area.

As someone who has for many years worked with the communities and gained experience in race and diversity practice, I want to bring these composite points to the table of other professionals. Practitioners and communities alike will understand that trying to change a big problem is frustrating. Whilst the work is often done at the individual level there is also benefit in placing the issues on the wider agenda to raise awareness and consciousness. So by raising the issues and making the links to generic application in tackling bigotry, the insights gained may be put to some good and general use.

A comment made during a focus group with professionals from the justice sector and Gypsies and Travellers struck me as particularly revealing. In the problem solving strategy, the discussions stated the problem, analysed it and sought solutions. In a moment of obviously rare inspiration one delegate exclaimed, 'Have you tried talking to one?' He was making a genuine attempt to seek a solution. This seemed to me to capture the problem.

It's hard to conceive of another group of people about whom such a comment might have been made. Perhaps in colonial India? The lack of incredulity amongst professional peers too was interesting, because the symbolic question was not seen as being out of place. There are echoes here of Michel Foucault's points on the construction of power, formalising exclusion and marginalisation of targeted groups at an institutionalised level (Foucault, 2000).

That pattern of almost institutionalised social taboo I found repeated in many circles; on several visits when discussions were held and trips made alongside Gypsies and Travellers, it was not uncommon that these represented their first visits to some prestigious places by the community. Although there was no formal apartheid in play, socially, perhaps there was. There were other accounts of more formal exclusion, with certain buildings openly displaying signs saying 'no dogs, no gypsies'. Just a sign, but illustrating a constructed hierarchy, in that order (MacGreil, 1996; Kenny, 1997).

The dialogue that exposes the two separate worlds of Gypsies and Travellers and of *gorgers* (non-Romany), is a curious one. Whilst Gypsies and Travellers may appear to keep themselves apart from the rest of society, it is more the case that society in general has not been over thirsty to learn and welcome these communities. Has there been an element of established comfort in the stereotypes, particularly in the negative and romantic ones that abound? As Paul (1998) explains, stereotyping forms an important aspect of rationalising through categories and labelling, and as such is natural. However, since positive images of Travellers are so rare and the popular media images and contemporary folklore predominantly so negative there is a tendency towards prejudice due to such imbalance (Morris, 2000a) to images that are institutionalised stereotypes.

Injecting the law into folklore shows that the two groups of Romany Gypsies and Irish Travellers are ethnic groups, defined by the Mandla criteria, and protected by Race Relations legislation in England and Wales. The first case supported by the Commission for Racial Equality (CRE) to assert that ethnic definition and provide legal protection was a long time coming. Romany

Gypsies were identified formally in 1989 (R v Dutton), and in an extension of the ruling Goldsmith formally identified Irish Travellers in 2000.

Given that the traceable history extends back centuries and that reference to Gypsies is included in legislation from 1530, the assertion of ethnic status seems to be the longest story of identity recognition in Europe. The stark situation is reinforced when you consider the reference sometimes made to England's oldest minority ethnic group, but the last to be recognised – and still to be accepted.

Setting out problem solving in this overlooked area, the evidence is that the situation and issues of Travellers have been missed, but offer insight into understanding the nature of prejudice itself. Travellers represent one of the most overt and resilient examples of prejudice, thus offering an opportunity to problem solve this most challenging area.

Understanding bigotry: symptoms and causes

Research indicates that in examining prejudice, emotion is involved in people's reasoning. So the problem practitioners face is emotional rather than simply rational. Essed (1991) makes the point that if tackling bigotry were merely a matter of stereotype correction, then doing so would be fairly straightforward.

Prejudice can be examined using cognitive psychology, specifically by assessing established neural networks and understanding behaviour modification (Meichenbaum, 1974). A social psychological understanding explains how perception is managed through established information processing networks (Reich and Adcock, 1986). Such cognitive processing has the potential to restrict alternative interpretations – it prevents you having an open mind. My research explored the theory and application of thinking styles on values and behaviour and susceptibility towards bigotry.

Thinking styles are important in problem solving. For example, if a person has well-established neural pathways restricting perceptions to mainly negative interpretations, it is the very process of their thinking that deserves exploration. Simply transmitting more information to such a person is unlikely to affect their views.

By taking a problem solving approach, practitioners can understand and work with the root of the problem and not just react to symptoms. Such an approach offers a wide variety of practical uses for practitioners (Augustine, 2004).

In a similar way to Dunning, Murphy and Williams's (1988) exploration of the roots of football hooliganism, the case study approach offers both specific and wider understanding. The situation of Irish Travellers and Romany Gypsies, whilst carrying quite specific contexts, also carry generic insights that can inform how practitioners might approach many aspects of bigotry. That the problem exists *within* the person carrying the bigotry links us to the conclusion that we need to understand what is happening before we can address bigotry.

By solving the specific problem we can generate generic solutions. One reason is that the problem lies with the bigot and not with the targeted group. We are able to work across different targeted groups since these are not where the problems lie. The processes behind bigotry are transferable. Simply to focus on stereotype reduction for one group would, amongst other failings, probably cause displacement to another target.

Listening with your eyes

My research reinforces the observation that victims are defined through the act of an offender, putting the power of definition in the hands of the offender.

By fully exploring the specific context of the communities involved from their perspective, the practitioner can acquire in depth emotional and rational understanding. If you trying to tackle bigotry you are seeking deep under-standing at the personal level: you are empathising with the emotional impact events can have on individuals. And the skills involved in gaining such insights require the building of trust.

In working with others to establish their specific context, you will develop *skills* that will provide you with a toolkit to address generic patterns of bigotry. Building trust is complex, but my research reflected the proposition that trust is built at the individual level and developed by *how* you are rather than *who* you are. One Gypsy delegate explained that they had become so saturated by rhetoric and empty promises that they no longer listened. They now judged people by what they actually did: they listened with their eyes.

In the next chapter we continue to work through the specific issues that appear to fuel disaffection and distance between practitioners and those experiencing oppression. It is possible, in thinking of the wider applications, to use the issues here as a case study. The communities can reveal insights which in turn help inform your underpinning knowledge. By the end of this book, we will be applying skills based on this understanding. The case study approach is replicable. I recommend forms of action research, utilising focus groups and similar, to explore and understand other complex social issues. Where there are mutual lessons to be learned, it can help if groups develop mutual understanding by working together. This process of group action learning helps build bridges through teamwork (Marsick *et al*, 2001).

What works: building on previous and recent work

From the work already carried out by researchers from various backgrounds such as criminologists, psychologists, educationalists, sociologists and historians, we can see some significant features that provide a useful foundation for our context. There has been a noticeable focus on training as a solution to the problem, and though I am critical of over reliance on a single method, previous work offers interesting findings to inform how the issues might be fully overcome.

The broad police diversity context firstly allows an insight into recent professional challenges. Police diversity trainers have identified in the past that the police training environment presents various challenges (Pizani Williams, 1994, Macpherson, 1999). This issue of *challenge* has been replicated in findings in international settings (Oakley, 1994; Pizani Williams, 1994; Chan, 1997) and has been recognised by HMIC (2003: 118), and Power (2004: 82-83). It is revealing that much of the existing literature is insular since many of the sources do not cross refer. Analysing the existing literature by taking a problem solving approach reveals silos. By their failure to link with other sources to form a complete picture such works become part of the problem rather than solution.

In the UK there is little acknowledgement of an international perspective and a general insular approach to police training which fails to link with wider discourses in antiracism. The Law Enforcement Aboriginal Diversity Network in Canada, for example, links training and policing practitioners with active community insight to improve understanding and mutually problem solve (Augustine, 2004). Such literature suggests that identification of eclectic best practice would offer development opportunities for practitioner development in the UK. In another innovative approach, the American Diversity Training Group have linked to community involvement to overcome student resistance and they portray this as a way for diversity trainers actively to 'give something back' to their own communities (Velasquez, 2004).

The dearth of links to wider professional discourse in the UK literature weakens any *holistic* findings. When mapped alongside each other, the international sources and accounts do corroborate with UK literature. The collective pattern shows consistently that trainers need the support of leaders or role models – in the police context in the workplace – to help develop change (ALTARF, 1984; Pizani Williams 1994; Mason 1999; Chan, 1997; Korhonen, 2004; Osler and Starkey, 2004). Without credible supporting structures to reinforce trainers' efforts, learning will be countered and probably undermined.

Since there appears to have been a lack of broad literature reviews for UK policing, there is no evidence of any examination of the relationship between police training and operations. Reviewing a wide source of international literature does offer more insight and revealing themes of challenge in training. These themes are explored in the next section.

The most difficult subject?

Pizani Williams (1994:16) identified the issues of Gypsies and Travellers as those which most trainers in police training found most difficult to address: a subject area which 'aroused extreme prejudice and hostility' in delegates. Conflict operates at both the hierarchical and personal levels. Conflicts are caused by organisational hierarchy or internal official power structures, represented by groupings of individuals or structures. But conflicts exist also at personal and cultural level, involving peer power.

Critical review of the practitioner focused literature reveals that these two themes have not been identified before. They help explore the problems facing practitioners, and categorise symptoms from causes. However, three points must be stressed. Firstly, at times themes may overlap with each other. Secondly, the organisational and personal share one overriding hallmark: they are negative and represent resistance. Finally, these themes are important, because they threaten to stop any progress being made by the practitioner towards treating Gypsies, or any minority groups, equitably.

Given the challenges of trying to change some long-held views, leadership and support is vital. Yet *Black Britain* (2004:1) reported on comments from the Police Diversity Trainers' Network, referring to 'harassment' of trainers. This harassment included bullying from senior police officers, 'because they regarded them as creating trouble'. A further source (*ibid*) explained 'Most trainers have suffered some form of harassment from superiors'.

The remit of the Police Diversity Trainers' Network established in 1999 by Nottinghamshire Police trainer Richard Martin, includes exchanging good practice between diversity trainers. The Network was established by practitioners and slowly attracted ACPO official support with a named ACPO port-folio holder appointed in 2003, David Westwood, then Chief Constable of Humberside. HMIC's *Diversity Matters* (2003) also made reference to the net-work and stated in Recommendation 7.5 (2003: 162) that ACPO and APA offi-cially recognise and support it as a formal Service-wide support mechanism.

That tension and conflict might exist between practitioners and senior managers is interesting particularly since the HMIC recommendation was officially to support the network. Fifty recommendations were made in the HMIC *Diversity Matters* report, (2003:157-165), and of these, 42 specifically cite Home Office, ACPO, Association of Police Authorities (APA), Police Train-ing and Development Board (PTDB) and Police Skills and Standards Organisa-tion (PSSO) (now termed *Skills for Justice*) to lead on development. The re-mainder of the recommendations all required ACPO officers at force level to implement them locally. No recommendations asked for practitioner action, only for them to be supported by others.

The Commission for Racial Equality began an inquiry in 2004 exploring why the *Diversity Matters* recommendations had not been fully complied with, a point also raised by the *Morris Inquiry* (2005). Further, HMIC identified in *Diversity Matters* a lack of senior management consistency in implementing diversity strategy, noting that, 'only commitment and leadership will achieve what is needed' (2003:45).

The issue of conflict and challenge is explicitly identified in the HMIC report. HMIC cite examples of 'real or perceived resistance, on the part of chief officers to race and diversity issues.' The report also states that a failure to support the issues would have a 'seriously detrimental effect' (2003:46). The context of *Diversity Matters* is also interesting, given its comments, in that this was the first major police service thematic inspection of race and diversity issues since Macpherson in 1999, which identified racism as an issue of un-paralleled importance for the police service to address.

Where *Diversity Matters* turns its focus on trainers, it notes that training can be seen by some as being 'removed from reality' and warns about this per-ception and its undermining effect. Further, the report discusses the need for diversity trainers to be 'resilient' because of potential ostracisation linked to their role, compounded by lack of support by management (2003:107). This point was repeated in the data I collected from trainers in focus groups. These issues are identified as so extreme that the potential for psychological damage is mentioned with reference to 'psychological risk assessments' (2003:118), not least because of pressure to 'walk the talk' (2003:107). The literature suggests that a lack of leadership in the *hierarchy* pushes a need for leadership amongst practitioners, but this creates a frustration of practitioner leadership without hierarchical power, or cultural support.

Power (2004:83) identifies amongst police diversity trainers a 'sandwich' scenario where a trainer noted that he 'found I was defending the Chief Constable... I have seen people getting very angry in training sessions.'

This was coupled with a trainer perception of a lack of support, resources or time to challenge embedded prejudice, a theme I also found strongly replicated in a pre-project focus group of diversity trainers (2004). Comparing the UK literature to Oakley's (1994) critique of the role of race and diversity training in Europe is also interesting. Examples from the Royal Dutch Police include a focus on changing culture in senior leaders as a prerequisite to affecting change and development. Korhonen's (2004) study comparing the UK with Finland is critical of the UK's tendency towards 'blanket' training and its failure to challenge internal working cultures through senior leadership.

Power (2004:86) identifies trends in police trainees, describing operational working practices concerning Gypsies and Travellers that were racist but driven by command level direction. Such accounts would cause the trainer some difficulty considering the apparent gulf between the messages from training and the priorities of the operational. Power (2004:87) describes a 'virus' of anti-Traveller racism in police culture, and refers to a police trainer 'guarantee' that the issues of racism towards Travellers emerge in any training since there is no 'political drive' to challenge such bigotry.

Korhonen's (2004) Finnish based work focused on the UK because of a presumption that given the background of the Stephen Lawrence Inquiry, the UK was 'advanced' in race and diversity training. Yet HMIC's (2003) report lists a large number of recommendations originating from Macpherson (1999) which have not been actioned. Ironically the international inquiries (Oakley, 1994; Korhonen, 2004) find the same shortfalls in UK training as HMIC identify.

Just because the UK has had a number of high profile cases of racial violence such as Stephen Lawrence's murder does not mean we have learned from the process. Given the context of the international literature, the UK may have more to learn from Europe. There seems to be no network of police diversity trainers across Europe, and the UK police training operates in isolation from other educational practitioners of adult education in the UK, and also from other policing practitioners. I also note that Oakley and Korhonen, despite producing works of real significance, have not effectively permeated police practitioner development in the UK.

So international comparison and critique by practitioners is conspicuous by its absence. The absence of literature is itself part of the problem in prac-titioner development. The practitioner voice needs to be heard much more clearly and to locate itself amongst other professional discourse.

Swimming against the tide

Black Britain (2004:1) reported that police trainers were working in training establishments where racist attitudes were widespread. An anonymous trainer reported that, 'I have felt less nervous dealing with violent situations and people with knives than I have going into a classroom'.

Several sources point to resistance by police officers towards diversity train-ing. Korhonen (2004) found it was common for delegates to interrupt or utterly refute to participate. The 'anti diversity' culture which Holdaway (1996) and Chan (1997) identify could be linked to Pettigrew's (1958) theories about dominant peer pressures based on a risk of exclusion. And culture and peer pressure could explain failings also in leadership.

Korhonen's (2004) Finnish report found much enthusiasm and passion amongst diversity trainers but a difficult working environment where police officers were very negative towards training and gave harsh and confronta-tional feedback. This made Korhonen question whether the training had any impact. The hostility of delegates is perhaps linked to 'self image' and dominant views (Reich and Adcock 1986), and Bancroft's (1999) theory of the stranger. Coupling the interpersonal level to group dynamics, Hewstone's (2002) 'in-group and out-group' theories offer some insight into why groups might be so hostile to difference. Looking at the cultural differences in UK police training, particularly concerning conflict, Korhonen concluded that there were aspects of the UK style in the Metropolitan Police which might be unsuitable for Finland. The problems Korhonen identified included two-day mandatory training and the apparent gap between training theory and operational practice.

Police training practitioners themselves seem to have few contacts with the Gypsy and Traveller communities. Consequently they have no positive grounded experiences with which to deal with student hostility and their assertions of negative views and values (Coxhead, 2003a).

As this whole area is under-researched, I explored the specific issue of attitudes in a pre-project questionnaire with the Police Diversity Trainers'

Network at their annual conference in 2003. This revealed that a majority of trainers wanted more professional development to help them perform effectively concerning Gypsy and Traveller issues and counter the anti locution they had experienced (Coxhead, 2003). In a pre-project focus group, views emerged that Gypsies and Travellers were perceived as the 'lowest tier in diversity' (Coxhead, 2005). A predominant issue in police occupational culture repeatedly showed itself: the powerful perceptions of Gypsies and Travellers as a criminogenic community (Power, 2004: 85). I found this trend important and worrying since this was an issue for not only trainers and trainees but police leadership.

Avoiding the issue: stealth racism

A final theme, though not one much cited in the police training focused literature, is the concept of 'stealth racism'. Philips (2004) identifies, as part of a CRE Inquiry, a phenomenon of delegates 'playing a game' around language, so masking their xenophobia and hatred towards races. This subterfuge in training events undermines any potential progress for real developmental change. In the BBC documentary *The Secret Policeman* (2003) an undercover journalist undergoing initial police training revealed extreme examples of racist language. Such overt racist views exist in only a minority but can tarnish the majority.

The pre-project questionnaire and focus group offer a contribution to the literature of stealth racism. Here, it was found that Gypsy and Traveller issues are an exception and that overt racism was still common. Overt prejudice makes it hard for trainers to deal with extreme manifestations of racism they may not have encountered before (Coxhead, 2003; 2004). The lack of literature about stealth racism in police training environments affirms the need for this book to expose the issue for practitioner development, using the case study of Gypsies and Travellers.

Practitioners who struggled with the overt nature of the prejudice concluded that people really had to meet face to face to overcome such strongly held views. Hewstone's (2002) theory of 'decategorisation', whereby learning is promoted as out-group members are encountered, seems relevant. On further discussion with practitioners, it was clear that much more understanding about the communities was needed. My early research (Coxhead, 2003) with the police diversity trainers' network where they met community members revealed this urgent need. Only by the structured meeting with Gypsies and Travellers at the conference were they able to identify their professional gaps in themselves. A similar in-group and out-group myth busting structured

meeting between training practitioners and Roma in Bulgaria was also successful (Tomova, 1999).

Psychological insights: how racists think

This section connects cognitive theories about the source and manifestation
of stereotyping and prejudice that is strongly resistant to change, with high
resistance areas to explore how pedagogical strategies try to apply theory. In
searching for parallels to this situation, I observed firstly that Gypsy and
Traveller issues are omitted within the discourse of antiracism training. This
was a part of the wider institutionalised discrimination – specifically exclusion – which confirmed the inadequate preparation for trainers regarding
Gypsies and Travellers.

Gundra, Jones and Kimberley (1986) note that in any high resistance area,
such as within racism and pedagogical strategies, the training practitioner
must have strong social and self-awareness. Racists can believe very strongly
that their labelling, categorisations and assumptions are the truth and such
strong belief can be overwhelming to a susceptible trainer. There is also a
weakness in transferring strategy to practice. The danger is that any strategy
will be ineffective in tackling racism unless practitioners have themselves
risen above value based labelling. No practitioner can be effective unless they
believe in what they are doing and their values are harmonised not cogni-
tively dissonant, with the content matter they are training.

In this same text, recommendations are made (1986:127) for equipping
teachers to deal more effectively with racism. This focuses upon attitudes to
minorities and the marginalisation of minorities but ironically mentions only
black people. I reflected that the understanding of automated unconscious
values within cognitive process will be largely unaffected by any didactic
input (Reich and Adcock, 1986: 98; Tomova, 1999: 29), and the training in any
case will be little use in equipping a practitioner to understand the cognitive
process of a racist in a group. Something far more powerful was needed to
stimulate change in the workplace.

Addressing racism against black people based on practitioner experience, a
London experiment (ALTARF, 1984) found that convincing pedagogical interventions recognised the unconscious cognitive process of prejudice and the
need to reinforce alternative social conditioning. Images around the school
buildings in the experiment were replaced and community links utilising
songs and crafts to celebrate community diversity forged a themed curriculum. This was reinforced by practical demonstrations of diversity: pupil

recruitment and staff recruitment, retention and progression. The technique was to provide an ethos of positive unconscious values that countered the social conditioning from outside. A similar pattern of labelling strategies for alternative role models is described by Hudack and Kihn (2001:147-156). Whilst I thought these techniques of positive action in social conditioning had some chance of success, I knew that in a training environment there was little time to create an alternative social culture. So changing behaviour in the long term depended critically on enough time being allocated to training, as well as the content and delivery.

Evaluating police training programmes concerning Gypsies in Hungary (Melykuti, 2000) revealed that long term professional development modular programmes worked better to overcome student resistance. Melykuti showed that 'spotlighting' Gypsies was not the best method, since the modules concerned generic work around community orientated policing which meant Gypsy issues were integrated and mainstreamed. Each module was introduced by a senior police officer. The evaluation of the programme indicated that this subtle entwining of the issues avoided negative conflict in the training.

Oakley (1999: 59-60) identified three approaches in police trainer training in the UK to address the high resistance to Gypsy and Traveller issues. The first was to provide cognitive information from an academic speaker, but this, although sometimes interesting, did not change stereotypes and attitudes. The second approach, to focus on prejudice through role-play, was seen as artificial, inauthentic, and provided no practical guidance on how to improve behaviour. The third approach involves not a lecture on cognitive information, but rather a Gypsy or Traveller themselves, 'speaking for I'. These sessions begin with delegates determining and asking questions which are answered in a learner directed session. Then the speaker presents their personal story to enhance the personal impact of the interaction. In my experience this approach works best, both in the power of 'speaking for I' and the flexibility and relevance offered by such interaction.

Oakley noted that 'host family interface' had been tried in many contexts but never with Gypsies and Travellers, and called for more work to develop community setting interaction. Failure to develop this approach in 1999 was attributed to lack of trust between community and police. Oakley reports success with other community groups in 'placement' activity, so we have to acknowledge that the problem lies with police/community relationship itself rather than with 'interface' methodology. This is relevant for contemporary developments for community placement within the Initial Police Learning and Development Programme (IPLDP, 2005).

The uniqueness of police occupational culture concerning 'commonsense' prejudice in operational policing is well documented (McConville *et al*, 1991; Holdaway, 2003). The literature also shows that the extreme manifestation relates to Gypsies and Travellers (Power, 2004: 83-84). Power describes a police trainee overtly expressing hatred of Travellers and that his views had been supported by trainers at training centre as 'okay'.

Walker (1984), in reviewing empiricism in learning theory, shows that the cognitive process is linked to contiguity in time and image association and that *experience* is necessary to facilitate both learning *and* changed performance. In a training activity the daily experience of social stigma needs to be countered by an alternative intervention but this is often restricted by the time allowed. Insufficient impact means there is no long term change in workplace performance. Focusing on workplace leadership shows itself as having far more influence in changing behaviours than training does.

Walker (1984) offers some examples of behaviour modification techniques, including cognitive modification with psychotic patients. He describes Ellis' (1962) rational emotive theory, which promotes self-acceptance and aware-ness but with an action plan for constructing a new cognitive map by affirma-tions of new visual states. Meichenbaum's (1974) self-instruction theories promote an extra 'cognitive loop' to consider 'what is expected or right?' and advises 'talking critically to the self' about actions rather than following spon-taneity. Wolpe's (1958) theory of thought stopping halts or freezes negative or inappropriate thoughts. The stopping can be done internally by the person or openly by the practitioner. I noticed an interesting parallel to this theory 'dis-covered' in 1999 by a police service diversity trainer to halt inappropriate comments. Rachman and Hodgson (1980), however, conclude that Wolpe's theory is unreliable.

All these techniques intercept the spontaneity of cognitive process in subject areas of high internal or external resistance. In short, an experience must then be linked to a frozen or diverted cognitive activity, away from any automatic route. Slowly, these techniques in parallel areas were providing me a list of requirements that my own strategies for training had to try and fulfil. I learned from Meyer (1979) and his experiments in behaviour modification and changing obsessive behaviour, rituals and expectations, that reinforce-ment and response prevention strategies outside the classroom, after training interventions, can be crucial to success. Rachman and Hodgson (1980) reported an 80 per cent success rate with such techniques, suggesting that such approaches were promising.

Harrop (1983) and Fox (1993) give pedagogical examples of attempts to modify behaviour and attitude. Techniques include intermixing reinforcement of the group contingent based on group and individual behaviour, common goal attainment, rules, praise, fines, modelling, exposure and counter reactance.

In these parallels of 'high resistance' there was recognition that when routine classroom reinforcers prove ineffective, alternatives must be found. It had been found in practical application that alternative, more powerful techniques had to be linked to territory association – it was more effective to take the technique to the person rather than take the person out of their environment to the technique. It seemed that I had to move my inquiry beyond the classroom.

Problem solving how to change behaviour using impactive interventions can be informed by considering views about teaching about the Holocaust. How is the Holocaust made a focus for strategies to provoke both intellectual and emotional responses about genocide? Burtonwood (2002) discusses the Holocaust as both a warning from history and a case study of how the 'normal moral framework' was abandoned. The enormity of the Holocaust makes it difficult to establish the best way to teach about it. In the moral framework argument, for example, it is considered that the events of genocide are so far removed from our normal moral basis that we cannot empathise or understand the events emotionally.

In training about Gypsies in Bulgaria, Tomova (1999: 29) found that straightforward correction of misinformation arising from stereotypes proved ineffective because the true facts were simply rejected by delegates. The focus on concentration camps and the terrible atrocities committed was powerful and delegates immediately stopped challenging and interrupting. Instead, their reaction was 'confusion'. A following session on role play around some of the horrific scenes of concentration camps increasingly prompted concern amongst delegates, who began to discuss issues personally with the trainer, raising newly identified concerns about their own prejudice. Tomova reported that this process had so much impact that some referrals for counselling were made afterwards because of the stress of self-confrontations about prejudice precipitated by the training.

Whilst acknowledging the difficulty of using the extreme model of the Holocaust, I linked a number of previously discussed theories together, placing the Holocaust at the centre as a pedagogical emotional catalyst. Burtonwood had discussed the 'bystander theory' as a problem as great as racism itself, and this set me thinking. Firstly Hewstone (2002), who shows that intergroup bias creates an 'in-group mentality' driven by ethnocentrism and social conformity, also discussed by Pettigrew (1958). Bigler (1999) considered racism a learned social cognitive process – a type of conditioning based on impactive experience and reinforcement. Adding to Bigler's theory and using Ellis's (1962), conclusions about the value of using a 'powerful experience' for change, a new cognitive map becomes possible as a learned social cognitive process Thus the individual might experience and reflect upon new alternatives to previous assumptions, which could break 'assumption cycles' as discussed by Meichenbaum (1974).

Direct challenge to a student, particularly one with dogmatic or authoritarian personalities, might be problematical so a possible way forward was to induce cognitive dissonance. Applying Star, Williams and Struffer's (1958) 'common enemy' theory, it occurred to me that the Holocaust offered itself as the 'common enemy'. Using this approach, with careful experiential learning reflection and debriefing, during and after the event, a new cognitive map could be drawn along with a member of an outsider group, in this case Gypsies and Travellers. The Gypsy Holocaust (Friedman, 1990) strengthened this construction.

Hewstone's (2002) theories on 'in and out-groups' combined with Star, Williams and Struffer's (1958) work on the process of team dynamics offers several practical possibilities. The process of team members working together may be even more important than the content of any activity. The process of simply working together helps develop mutual understanding. The use of this application for team building to overcome bigotry is aided by insights in sports performance and psychology (Cox, 1998; Schmidt and Wrisberg, 2000). I return to this application in Chapter Seven.

Aside from content and methodology, the central issue of the calibre of the trainers is clear in the literature. The complexity of issues and the skills required of a trainer to manage these various issues in high resistance environment was recognised by Oakley (1999), based on his extensive experience of police trainer training at the Home Office Centre, Turvey. The Turvey Programme (1999) noted that the Gypsy Traveller issue was particularly a matter of concern for trainers given the high levels of distrust, and the nature of overt racism towards these communities. The Turvey Programme identified that these factors called for high levels of special skills and personal qualities. Particular sessions could be so intense that it was preferable that issues were mainstreamed into wider diversity programmes, and not delivered in isolation.

Clearly, training has limits in changing established social conditioning. In the next chapter I explore the apparent symbolic divide between these 'in-groups' and 'out-groups', asking 'why?'

Summary

- Romany Gypsies and Irish Travellers should be recognised as distinct ethnic groups

- Prejudice toward Gypsies and Travellers can provide insight into generic lessons about tackling all prejudice

- Prejudice for Travellers means being seen as 'less than equals'

- Prejudice can become 'normalised' by the dominant group(s) so that the problem goes unrecognised

- Correcting stereotypes is not enough to change people's long-held views

- One of the greatest challenges is to eradicate the overt stereotypes that have prevailed for so long about Travellers

- The dearth of positive interaction has kept Travellers an out-group

- Racism is not inborn, it is a learned social cognitive process

- Programmes to overcome prejudice are more successful when they are mainstreamed and can be maintained

3

Them and Us

'The police are not our police,' a young Irish Traveller told me. Although there is always a concern over replicability and representation in an ethnographic insight of this kind, there is also directness and personal honesty. In light of the social history outlined in Chapter Two, the comment is not surprising. Her words capture the reality that exists today that without action nothing will change and is being carried for future generations. The delegates to the two focus groups spoke openly, notwithstanding the mix of police and Gypsies (see page 12).

The police and prejudice

The data revealed enduring patterns of prejudice. Gypsies and Travellers directed hatred at police personnel and there were reciprocal expressions from the police towards the communities. The social and cultural distance between the communities and the police is maintained by powerful negative perceptions. As one police officer said: 'Prejudice towards Travellers in the police is not only accepted, it's expected'.

This comment not only gives insight into popular views but also exposes a workplace pressure to conform and collude with negative attitudes. It reveals a culturally institutionalised norm, where the peer pressure is *misleading* rather than leading professional ethics and integrity. The link to other commentaries about in-groups and out-groups, group dynamics and peer pressures help locate the existing prejudice towards Travellers within wider analysis of the police culture (O'Brien *et al*, 2000, Davies and Thomas, 2004). The Irish Traveller's comment illustrates the theories of bigotry discussed earlier. And crucially, it exists now.

The overt nature of racism toward Travellers exposes viewpoints that are not so readily found aimed at other ethnic groups. The following quote expresses the view Travellers are an interesting barometer of the reality of people's views, suggesting there is a reluctance or fear to speak openly about other groups.

> We all have prejudices but we know that it is not acceptable to express them or use this language, so you don't know the extent of real prejudice. But, with Travellers this isn't the case and people will express it openly.

At the conference of Travellers and police, one Traveller identified the overt nature of prejudice towards Travellers as 'back door racism, a group that gives a focus for prejudice'. Travellers and Gypsies are a socially acceptable opening for bigotry to surface. More respect seems to be afforded to some racial groups than others – a pecking order of racism. He questioned whether genuine equality is given to all ethnic groups: 'If we talked about and treated all black people the way we treat Gypsies would this be acceptable?'

As another said:

> A lot of people still view Gypsies and Travellers as subhuman and treating them as such is seen as some sort of achievement that should be bragged about.

This insight reinforces how deep prejudice is. Clearly superficial work such as 'stereotype correction' will achieve very little. The notion of 'trophy prejudice' suggests not just a predisposition for prejudice but a thirst and glory for it.

One police representative drew a comparison between attitudes towards Travellers as a form of demonisation (Cohen, 1971, 2002) and the theories of in-groups and out-groups (Hewstone, 2002): 'Once people start using 'them' to describe Travellers it immediately dehumanises them.'

This is the danger of social demonisation (Cohen, 1971, 2002). It generates a downward cycle of social scapegoating, where people get what they choose to look for in others (Rosenthal and Jacobson, 1968; Rosenthal and Rosnow, 1991).

Prejudice appears to operate a continuum of social positioning from active pursuance to complicity and lack of challenge. Absence of challenge is a form of negative acquiescence – the ethos reinforces the prejudice and supports a form of consistent propaganda. The comment of one police officer illustrates the comfortableness of media prejudice towards Travellers, itself a symptom of the generalised support of the prejudice: 'People still feel comfortable to say racist things about Travellers; the media is comfortable to say these things.'

We can see here how ethical positions are sometimes peer and culturally rather than individually led. Given a cultural anchor amongst peers which is pervasive, how many individuals make up their own minds and how many follow the crowd? Would it matter which way the crowd was going? Mainstreaming prejudice makes it difficult to redress individual perceptions proactively if peer pressure is negative.

Why?

So why is prejudice against Gypsies and Travellers so ingrained? The community felt there was a distance between the police and the community which was underpinned by fear and repeated negative experience.

One community delegate described a conversation with a police recruit:

> I asked them, if house dwellers phone and complain about Travellers 'what do you do?' The officer said 'we put our armour on'. There are myths about violence. I think the police are frightened.

The automatic reply of the officer speaks volumes. The following comment may cast light on it: 'Ninety nine per cent of contact with Gypsies and Travellers is negative.'

Self fulfilling prophecies (Rosenthal and Jacobson, 1968) explain such cyclical thinking. It is important not to dismiss or judge views, but rather to try to analyse and understand them. Is paramilitary and over zealous policing the root? Is anti-police feeling amongst Travellers the cause? A history of distance between the groups has locked the perceptions of both parties. The need for proactive dialogue and interaction would be an obvious way of breaking the stalemate of 99 per cent negative experience. And why is the situation different regarding other groups?

To judge from this Traveller's account, abnormality defines the Traveller experience.

> The police get a warrant to a site to search a whole Gypsy site. It would not happen on a council estate. People would not tolerate it. Sealing off entire sites to catch a criminal – would they seal off a council estate for the same thing?

It was said that the police were above the law and that Traveller and Gypsy people had no place to turn in the imbalance of power against them.

> My lad was taken into a police van and beaten up. If he had been badly injured who would have been responsible? Not the police.

The research also revealed a strong view amongst the Gypsy community which one of them summed up thus: 'When police forces are held to account it is not filtering through to Gypsy communities.'

A community delegate relates how the police did not respond to calls for engagement, saying:

> The rhetoric does not result in action. My local force will not turn up at meetings or give a response or engagement. We've put a complaint in and nothing happened.

The first steps towards dialogue are bound to be difficult for all concerned. Police personnel might well feel unwelcome when they make efforts towards positive engagement. Perceptions are difficult to measure quantitatively so if there is an underlying feeling of hostility, the smallest upset is interpreted in the worst way. The negative cycle needs to be broken before positive interaction and trust can develop.

Within my research focus groups policing operations were discussed. Over policing, particularly at funerals, weddings and site evictions was a consistent pattern. Weddings and funerals in particular were family events that they said attracted the police as 'operations' and 'intelligence gathering opportunities'. A community delegate reported that:

> The handling of funerals is terrible. Police stopping cars of people going to pay respect being stopped to check on tax – there is no understanding of the grieving and culture. When operations have been carried out it's because Gypsies are a target.

To him, policing operations seek an excuse to gather intelligence, and large family events offer opportunities. Gypsies are a target because they are Gypsies, not because there is a funeral – a perception that it's not about the 'what' but about the 'who'.

Policing personnel contributed to this discussion, recounting cases of policing incidents being titled simply 'Gypsies' or 'Itinerants', as if this were self explanatory. The perceptions in the views expressed are real enough and we have to understand the issues and look for solutions.

The research found that paramilitary policing style was particularly evident at large funerals and site evictions. Evictions were flashpoints for both community and police, driven by an accommodation issue but sometimes ending with the police using riot shields and CS gas. The increased use of council employed bailiffs did not hide the role of the police in creating images that lasted for years, damaging any positive relationship:

> When bailiffs go on site the police have to be there. The bailiffs are playing the police. The bailiffs are paid and love it but the young people – they see the police.

The subliminal message in this comment is that the legitimacy and integrity of policing is in question. The complex nature of legitimate policing means that a police presence can signify tacit approval even when it is the bailiffs who are acting. Trust, accountability and consensus can only be built if account is taken of people's perceptions.

Locating the specific insights raised here within wider critical examination of policing styles (Findlay and Zvekic, 1993), I wondered whether there is a causal link between the perception of paramilitary style policing and changes in policing over the last few decades. Jefferson (1990) draws attention to the trends of enforcement demonstrated in the Miners' Strike, football match and demonstration policing and the relationship generally between public control, the Public Order Act and emergent policing tactics. Although mainstream community policing styles have now permeated most areas of police work it seems not to be the case for Travellers.

To judge from the perceptions of the community members involved in my research, ordinary events are regularly made extraordinary by the intervention of authority. They see large scale evictions in which the police are their enemy and this is corroborated by the confrontational style of mundane contacts. As one Gypsy observed:

> The early Gypsy experience, by young children, is of police kicking our churns over and making us move on. It is the 21st century and we need to stand back and look at true community policing.

They had come to feel that if no one cares, there's no one left to report things to; you can only expose a problem if someone, anyone, will acknowledge your voice. During the research process, the normalisation and resigned acceptance of the disdain of the police seemed to shock non-community delegates who were hearing about the community's experiences for the first time.

Over policing and under protecting?

To explore the motives and perceptions further one must know the background context. What is happening is not simply co-incidental, spontaneous or unconnected.

A policing delegate told how he had been introduced to Travellers operationally with suggestions that Travellers needed virtual 'reservation' style policing:

> I was taken for a ride out as part of getting to know the area, and taken out in a riot van. I was taken down to a site in this riot van and the officers were surprised to get a negative reaction when they dropped in for a chat in a riot van.

This reflects policing culture particularly and hazing and initiation rites more generally (Nuwer, 1999; Brown and Campbell, 2004). This is confirmed by another delegate's description of the policing of Travellers and Gypsies:

> Gypsy sites are seen as a ghetto so taking young officers out onto sites is seen as a badge of honour showing that they are not frightened to go onto sites.

Such pervasive cultural dimensions reinforce the importance of workplace Principle Centered Leadership, as Simon Leckie points out in Chapter One.

Police officers, too, rated their experience 'Ninety nine per cent negative'. The pattern of confrontation and enforcement focus, with no evidence of community policing, was illustrated and confirmed by a catalogue of bad experiences as the outcome. It is vital that the backdrop of distrust and alienation informs problem solving, even though much of the distrust is based on perceptions.

The background reading for police training in race and diversity studies makes frequent reference to policing by consent, and the notions of integrity and legitimacy in policing (Scarman, 1981; Alderson, 2004). The combination of disadvantaged youth and perceptions of zealous police targeting was shown to have precipitated serious disturbances. Scarman urged a 'lessons learned' re-emphasis on neighbourhood policing principles. Yet the pattern of disenfranchised and angry resentment seemed as strong as ever concerning Travellers. Like black youth in Brixton, they 'had had enough'. But although everyone knew action was needed, they were frustrated. They did not know how to overcome the perceived barriers and take the next step in bridging the gap.

Cultural awareness training was seen as one way of dealing with the lack of knowledge of community policing teams. Cultural awareness training does contribute in certain contexts in reducing specific tensions in the policing relationship. One officer pointed out:

> When was the last time you sent a dog into a Mosque? We don't do that. Well, why do you put dogs into a trailer?

This addresses the lack of respect or understanding shown towards Travellers by the police. One officer highlighted their ignorance, saying:

> We're not aware of Gypsy and Traveller issues ...it's not seen as racism.

But it is a result of the total non-recognition of the issues – a form of social invisibility. Omission, like silence, speaks volumes (Mason, 1999). There is ratification at the political level in cases of racism. Specifically, legislation concerning Gypsies and Travellers is unhelpful since the definition in Planning Law is distinct from the Race Relations criteria. We have seen that there is a unique criterion to 'prove' identity before certain rights are afforded. This further confounds the straightforward recognition of Traveller and Gypsy identities.

Other incidents suggested that the attitude of agencies towards Travellers was simple belligerence, such as this:

> A police officer was on my land in the middle of the night. I asked him what he was doing. He wouldn't answer the question but before he left he said 'I will remember you.'

The national problem of stop search and stop encounter monitoring has been exposed by Dawson (2006). His independent research is in the absence of any Home Office monitoring. More work is needed as it would help establish more normalised policing for Travellers – i.e. the same services and accountability mechanisms would apply to Travellers as to other ethnic groups.

Regarding Travellers as the enemy and all Travellers as criminals impeded the work of the police in dealing with actual criminals. One community delegate condemned the generalisations made by the police about a whole community:

> A lot of police seem to believe that all Travellers are 'at it' and are involved in drugs etc. Most Travellers want to see such people arrested. The police go for the soft option and go onto sites rather tackle the serious criminals.

Police activity was not only missing the target but also alienating a large population. This was more important to Travellers than, for example, 'No Gypsy' signs on pub doors. A delegate explained that there were fundamental issues that needed tackling, and that fundamentals not symptoms should be the priority.

There seemed to be an opportunity for the police to engage with the community to work at problem solving, but this would be difficult until the negative generalisations were challenged and overcome. After some discussion, the Gypsy delegates concluded that stereotyping may have resulted in some good arrests, but that '... many innocent people had got caught in that net'.

A key finding in my research was that specific issues could be resolved through dialogue, but that this required a leap of faith to leave behind assumptions and work with the communities on common ground. The mutual mistrust was the product of the failure to even begin policing by consent and policing through dialogue. It had not so much broken down as never started – a shocking indictment of 21st century policing in Britain.

There was a cry for action so that future generations would not be in the same predicament – 'I'm not here for me, I'm here for my grandchildren', said one community delegate. A focus on the youth of tomorrow does offer a positive focus, although generational change takes time, maybe too much time. The need to break the cycle of distrust and distance from the police is paramount. One Traveller made the point clearly:

> What do Travellers really think of the police? Travellers don't report because they don't trust the police. Just what can be done to make Travellers trust the police?

Much of the literature, from Scarman (1981) onwards has emphasised the need rather than merely the desire to work in consensual relationships with communities to achieve effective policing. As Townshend (1994) put it, 'An armoured tank never achieved much in policing'. Recent strategies towards consensual policing have operated at the strategic level rather than in practice. More local 'person to person' trust building is needed. Evidence supporting the need to work with communities is overwhelming. Danflous (2007) notes a parallel need on a pan-European scale to improve the relationship between policing and Roma. What is clear is the need to apply existing principle of consensual policing in the work with Gypsies and Travellers.

Police practitioners and community members reading this book will recognise both the specific and generic issues raised here and reflected in the quotes. I have found parallel views amongst other community groups, indicating the urgent need for authentic inclusion. The findings described here can hopefully help us to tackle these important issues for everyone's benefit.

Combining the research process with the bringing together of the two groups concerned presented a unique opportunity to get to grips with the issues and determine what needs to be done. It offers a model for use within general applied practice. Accessing community voices unleashed authenticity and a thirst to not waste the potential in addressing policing fundamentals that had escaped the sophisticated development in other areas of policing. What the study revealed was the paramount importance of breaking the cycle of mutual suspicion and mistrust – but also a genuine desire to make positive changes.

Summary

- The whole issue of racism towards Travellers has long been overlooked

- The uniquely overt nature of prejudice towards Travellers offers insight into the nature of bigotry itself

- Progress is being marred by a negative cycle of mutual distrust between the communities and the justice system

- The desire for positive change is clear, and can be achieved by stopping abnormal practices towards Travellers

- It is vital for future generations that the past does not go on repeating itself

4

The Nature of Prejudice

This chapter outlines the analysis stage of the research within its problem solving approach. It considers a range of issues, from overt stereotyping to the limits of what training alone can achieve. It analyses the depth of the problem and the four key themes that illustrate essential areas for the practitioner to address when seeking to improve practice.

Overt stereotyping

The first research theme was overt stereotyping. Students defended the overt display of antilocution on the grounds that stereotyping 'helps catch criminals'. How deeply these views were entrenched was evident from the way stereotypes were seen not as stereotypes but as facts. We know that correcting stereotypes is ineffective in changing views (Tomova, 1999: 29). There is no simple 'correction' to be made; indeed the complexity of the issue has been underestimated. Discussions about stereotypes as a generic topic are a standard component of diversity training amongst police officers (Coxhead, 2004). My findings reinforced the need for greater professional understanding, as stereotypes were extremely powerful and influential in workplace culture. There was a need for deeper analysis of stereotyping. Relating the literature on stereotyping to accounts of the experience of prejudice offers new insights for improving professional practice.

Overt stereotyping had soon come to light in my pre-project research questionnaire findings. The questionnaires revealed widespread overt negative views amongst students and a stubborn resistance to altering them. Students refused to listen to any information about Gypsies and Travellers, maintaining that the stereotypes were not stereotypes but facts.

Curiously, stereotypes were seen in two ways. Firstly, that the stereotype was fact and a negative one at that – one student summed it up by saying that: 'Gypsies and Travellers are all criminals'.

Yet they also recognised the existence of stereotyping: 'If there's no inter-action, [it] leads to problems. We need to break down the stereotypes'. This was strange, when they believed that they knew all about Gypsies and Travellers. But saying they needed to overcome stereotypical thinking by tackling the lack of interaction suggested that they recognised they didn't know the facts. This notion of 'knowing' might explain some of the students' resistance to any alternative information.

In the questionnaire findings, practitioners added free text about their views on the challenges in overcoming stereotypes and the difficulties for trainers. They admitted that they themselves were ill equipped to counter the stereo-types and needed to engage with Gypsies and Travellers to find out more. Sixty five per cent of the respondents stated that they did not feel profes-sionally equipped to deal with student attitudes towards Gypsies and Travel-lers. In the focus groups the same issues appeared, with the clear message that racism towards Travellers is overt.

> We all have prejudices but we know that it is not acceptable to express them or use this language so you don't know the extent of the prejudice. But with Travellers this isn't the case and people will express it openly.

There are two important and distinct issues: the overt nature of the anti-locution and the stereotyping itself. Overt because views are articulated, even volunteered, and because of the strong, almost aggressive, resistance to dis-cussing matters. The overt resistance also seems linked to a group response that left the trainer so isolated that the issues were not addressed properly. The comments are telling:

> I would go further than that – prejudice against Travellers is not only acceptable in the force, it is expected. On a course I was on an officer from a small middle class village who was positive about Travellers had been attacked by the majority of the group.

The second issue concerns the nature of the stereotypes, the myths, repre-sentations and images. This mixing of the certainty that Gypsies and Travellers were trouble whilst also seeing them as strangers is illogical and irrational. While the negative views were expressed overtly, training prac-titioners had difficulty countering students' certainty and their fear of the unknown. As one observed:

> But if you don't have role models you have difficulties because if you ask people if all Gypsies conform to the stereotypes of them most will simply say yes they do.

The entrenched attitudes were dominant even when a Traveller was involved in the session:

> When I've been in to do training, there was an attitude towards us. The only questions any one asked were about council tax or small piles of rubbish. They did not want to engage in questions.

The overtness of this racism is remarkable. It flies in the face of race relations as documented in the Scarman report in 1981 through to Macpherson in 1999 (Rowe, 2004) and lately from inquiries led by Morris (2005) and the CRE (2005). Rowe suggests that race issues have been driven underground because of the high profile of Macpherson. One reaction has been political correctness – the notion that people cannot openly express themselves and freeze amidst the issues (*Police Review*, 25th March 2005). Police are afraid to discuss issues of race lest they breach discipline codes. In a cultural ethos such as this, training events on diversity issues are inhibited. Yet any such guardedness fell away when the subject was Gypsies and Travellers. The racism was blatant and all-pervasive. One delegate said:

> I was involved in some training and when you mention Travellers it's like lighting touch paper, and as a trainer, I could not get beyond that.

Racism may have become more covert towards other groups but this is not true for Travellers and Gypsies, about whom negative views were expected. One delegate offered an explanation: 'I think people need their fix of racism. I think they are aware of legislation. '

Psychological profiling and tendencies towards authoritarian personalities might offer some insight here. More research is required to explore the whole issue of 'scapegoating dependency' in occupational working cultures, building on Rachman and Hodgson's (1980) work on obsessions and compulsions and the interventions made by Pettigrew (1958) and Meichenbaum (1974).

Gypsies and Travellers are an accepted target for hatred, justified by the stereotyped representations and images as an out-group. Membership of an out-group (Hewstone, 2002) is defined by references to their being different to the in-group. Comments expose the inherent desire to see the other adjust to some concept of ethnocentric 'normality'. Typical was the remark: 'I always wondered why Gypsies didn't buy a house like everyone else.'

Thus Travellers and Gypsies are identified not by the attributes of their culture but by being different to the assumed positive values of the in-group who they are not. It follows that there was little interest in Gypsy and Traveller cultures. What matters to these officers is that they are different. This resonates with the work of Hewstone (2002) and Reich and Adcock (1986), which found that out-groups are targeted because of their difference.

As one senior police officer acknowledged,

> It's been missed; the whole thing's been missed. In twenty-five years of policing I can't ever recall being asked to consider Travellers.

The notion of invisibility as discussed by O'Nions (1995), Acton, (1998) and Hancock (2002) connects with commentaries of the 'Gypsy problem' outlined in Chapter Two. The alternative to invisibility is the appearance of Gypsies and Travellers as a problem. These attitudes help explain why Gypsies and Travellers are disliked, why so little effort is made to understand the issues and why the problem is blamed on them rather than seen as racism. Anti-gypsyism promotes negative resistance to any positive value of Travellers (Hancock, 2002:53).

The generic patterns of racism fluctuate, defined by what we choose to identify. As Hesse (1993:11) put it: 'Racism always seems to be with us, but not solely in the same places where we traditionally look.'

My research found that stereotypes were based on myths and fear of the unknown. When Gypsies and Travellers did attend training events the reaction among the police was that they did not fit the stereotype. It didn't help that, as one officer said, 'The problem is that many officers have already been exposed to old school stereotypes.'

Media images confirm the negative views: 'It's the stereotyping that is the problem, it is building up again, and it is sustained by the press'.

On the subject of community cohesion, the community delegates mentioned past tensions between English and Irish Travellers, but reported that 'things are changing. Irish and English Travellers are uniting to protect their communities'.

In the case of black racism (Singh, 1993; Holdaway, 1996; Mason, 1999) reference is consistently to skin colour so race is associated with appearance. Yet Gypsies and Travellers seemed to be identified by their behaviour. Because this behaviour is seen negatively the defining label of 'Gypsy' equates to 'problem', as described by this Traveller:

> We don't talk about a black problem or the immigrant problem but we still talk about the Gypsy problem. Gypsies are UK citizens that have fought and given service for this country.

The theme of stereotyping adds to previous literature in several ways. Firstly, it conjoins the discussion of anti-gypsyism (Hancock, 2002) with Hewstone's references to 'out-groups' (2002) and shows how this outlook is linked to resistance to change. This shows anti-gypsyism as an active and overt state rather than as passive ignorance. Actively maintaining an out-group requires both action and inaction to maintain negative status for the out-group. The *failure* to challenge racism is an act: a decision not to challenge. And this was particular to Gypsies and Travellers:

> Officers will challenge language such as 'Paki' and maybe gay prejudice but not prejudice against Gypsies.

Evidence of such stubborn labelling comes from policing practitioners. Police trainers found they were challenged by students when they offered alternatives to the students' opinions that all Travellers were criminals. This trainer said it was common that 'Police officers state all Gypsies are thieves and they will not alter their views even when challenged by trainers'. He explained that student resistance to balanced debate is immense and finished by saying 'I don't normally deliver training but it was so bad that I walked out a shaken man, to be honest'.

Any notion that this prejudice is based on simple ignorance is confounded by the fierce resistance that was evidenced. What is clear is that anti-Gypsy racism is *active* even in inaction and highly resistant to challenge through discussion. The police students were rehearsed in theories of prejudice and discrimination, but they saw this group as different and as outside such concepts.

These embedded views are the reason why the police service has abandoned the protection and respect they afford to other minority groups. It brought into question previous diversity training. Perhaps all we have learned is which groups have some power and status and which have none. I move therefore to the subject of identity and hierarchy.

Identity and hierarchy

The research uncovered a hierarchy of diversity – with Gypsies and Travellers at the bottom. Travellers represent a last bastion of racism because of the groups' status. In practical terms, despite much effort to outlaw all racism, racism towards Gypsies remains acceptable. The picture is of Travellers as a disenfranchised group, missed out of the legal recognition and protection they should have (CRE, 2004). It appears that Travellers' lack of power creates an opportunity for racists freely to express their views. Trainers found it difficult to conduct rational discussions with students because of a student pack mentality allowing Travellers to be treated as legitimate targets.

One significant way that Gypsy identity is pushed to the bottom of the power hierarchy is through denying the existence of racism. One justice worker asserted that it was vital 'not to lose sight it's a race issue – we need to in-fluence practitioners out there'. One reason for the non-recognition of Gypsies and Travellers was a blurring of white European ethnicity. As one Gypsy explained, 'the figures are buried in white European ethnicity, it's not seen as racism'.

The legislation in the UK is confusing and unhelpful. There are two defini-tions of who a Gypsy is. Firstly, there is the 'gypsy' (note lower case) used in Planning Law. Secondly, there is the Race Relations definition of Romany Gypsy and Irish Traveller, which was informed by Mandla v Dowell Lee (1983). The Mandla Criteria importantly defines a set of criteria for ethnicity based on aspects of history, culture and shared language and then legally protects these groups. The situation of having different definitions of Gypsy identity based on which type of court is presiding is more than unenviable – it is a unique legal situation for any ethnic group in Europe. Many readers will be unaware of this legal anomaly, yet Travellers and Gypsies referred to this problem consistently as having enormous effect in undermining their heri-tage and racial status.

Ironically, in policing practice, it is clear that Gypsies and Travellers are identi-fied, but only based on stereotypes of – usually criminal – activity, as the police comment that 'Gypsies and Travellers are all criminals' illustrates. Evidence of this same point is replicated in Power (2004) and Dawson (2006).

There were discussions about how mechanisms could support the imple-mentation of Race Equality Schemes, dealing with racist incidents, and the Race Relations (Amendment) Act. Yet there was a frustrating problem that these mechanisms were not activated because there was so little recognition of the racial status of Travellers. A Traveller spoke about victimisation: 'Travel-lers are not reporting crime, it's hidden, there's no confidence to report crime.'

The repeated reference to the fact that crimes against them are not reported by Travellers and that 'the police do not see us as victims' suggests an institu-tionalised norm was considered by some police delegates for the very first time in the focus groups. One police officer remarked that 'In twenty-five years of policing I can't recall when I've been caused to engage in the Gypsy Traveller issues'.

Another officer conceded that the recognition of Travellers and Gypsies as communities 'has not sunk in at the force level'. One reason for this was offered by a police officer who maintained that the traditions of previous decades still dominated modern policing:

> Comments and jokes about Travellers and tarmac are common. The problem is that senior officers of today were young bobbies 30 years ago when the accepted practice was to throw bricks at caravans until the Gypsies moved on.

This vicious circle means that there is no recognition of the problem and no impetus for police action to improve, since the whole situation remains hidden. One Gypsy stated that where victim reporting does occur, problems in classification mean the problem still remains invisible, so that 'Gypsy and Traveller issues are not being recorded as racist incidents.' The Stephen Lawrence report defines a racist incident as 'any incident that is considered to be racist by any person' (Macpherson, 1999). The problem is not in Statute or guidance but in application and practice. In short there is no excuse for failing to recognise Gypsies and Travellers.

Yet, as my research reveals, the problem exists and is serious.

> We had an elderly lady who was firebombed, police said 'we didn't lodge it as a racist incident because the old lady didn't look like a Gypsy'. They did not investigate because they said 'you know what it is like, it will just be one family having a go at another one'.

Gypsies felt stigmatised and hated by other communities and they are left to 'look after their own'. As one said:

> At the moment we are not viewed as a community – we are viewed as a nuisance. Travellers are a close knit community and that has strengths and weaknesses. My child does not tell friends she is a Traveller because of people's bad reaction. People need to see Travellers as a community not a problem.

A Traveller pointed out:

> In order to engage Gypsy Traveller community the first step is to acknowledge there are racially motivated crimes and record them as such.

Two significant cases illustrate how non-recognition prevents justice for Gypsies and Travellers. Irish Traveller Johnny Delaney was fifteen years old when he was murdered in Cheshire in 2003. The police treated the killing as a racially motivated attack but in the Crown Court there was no formal acceptance that the death was due to racism. His father, Patrick Delaney began a campaign to improve criminal justice in what the Traveller community has referred to as 'our Stephen Lawrence'.

In 2003 an effigy of a caravan with Gypsy children inside was burnt as part of a publicly funded bonfire celebration in Firle, Sussex. This was investigated by the police and commented upon by the Commission for Racial Equality but the Crown Prosecution Service decided on taking no further action on charges of incitement to racial hatred. The events in Firle received press coverage in some tabloid newspapers at the time which portrayed the arson as harmless fun.

Community representatives said that both these important cases had implications at national level. 'We've had Johnny Delaney and Firle. We need judicial level inquiries.' The communities' frustration was immense: 'Just what does it take to bring about change?'

A justice worker lamented that change is too often slow and prompted by extreme need. 'It is a horrible thing to say but all the things that have pushed the police on have been either demonstrations or a tragedy.' A Gypsy pointed out that these issues have been discussed repeatedly and that the community was calling for improvement as long as 'twenty years ago'. It was inexcusable – 'something must be done or we'll still be here in another twenty years'.

Another Traveller made clear that the murder of Johnny Delaney, and the long history of injustice meant that change was urgent: 'We need action now. We cannot afford to wait; there is a need for action now.' The depth of feeling and anger is intense. It is imperative that workers in criminal justice address the issues quickly before Traveller confidence dissipates any further or their disaffection turns to anger:

> Gypsies are very passive and compassionate but compassion can spill out into anger. Other groups have become accepted but Travellers have not. Travellers are peaceful and are not aggressive and have never rioted in 600 years. Maybe they should.

My view is that the bigotry we see aimed at Travellers is part of some bigger need for scapegoats. As one police officer candidly remarked: 'If we're saying these things and we shouldn't have a go at Travellers, then who can we have a go at?' This revealing question exposes an alarming psychological profile. Skolnick (1994) and Reiner (2000) identify generic patterns of machismo and racial prejudice in police culture as an underlying problem in police attitudes. As a practitioner researcher I was concerned about the serious problem in police culture and feared that promoting respect for Travellers could just cause targeting to be transferred to another out-group. Investigating this last bastion of racism offers an important opportunity to challenge not only racism towards Travellers but also the underlying conditions in which bigotry of all kinds flourishes.

Enemies but strangers

The third theme I identified was the paradoxical view held by the police service of Gypsies and Travellers as the 'enemy' of, and yet 'stranger' to them. A police officer reflected the norms of institutional and police culture towards Travellers when he said:

> In our work we are not going to come into contact with law abiding Travellers... police officers are still happy to talk about pikeys and Gypos.

Gypsies recounted how they are treated differently to other communities, for instance:

> The police get a warrant to a site to search a whole Gypsy site. It would not happen on a council estate. People would not tolerate it. Sealing off entire sites to catch a criminal – would they seal off a council estate for the same thing?

The same speaker warned that routine police behaviour was intrusive and aggressive, making the community continue to hate the police, so influencing future generations of Travellers.

> Police go onto sites to check fuel and that. They tend to provoke the young people until they get a reaction. Officers from a PSU went onto our site and let off fire-crackers. These things are normal.

The enmity between the police and Gypsies means policing is used only as enforcement against them. As a justice worker observed 'The view that Travellers do not have the right to fair and equal policing is worrying' that is confirmed by a Traveller 'we're policed as a problem, not a community.'

Police officers acknowledged that police interaction with Gypsies was 'ninety-nine per cent negative'. This pattern of confrontation and enforcement – the antithesis of community policing – is illustrated in this account from a Gypsy of a routine vehicle stop:

> I know a situation where a police officer couldn't find anything wrong with a Traveller's car so the policeman got annoyed and said, 'If I had my way I'd leave you lying in the ditch'.

Many background studies that are generally covered in police training on race and diversity emphasise policing by consent and the recommendations of the Scarman Report of 1981. The mix of disadvantaged youth and over zealous policing caused serious disturbances and Scarman emphasised the need to operate principles of neighbourhood policing. The same themes of disenfranchisement and furious resentment seemed just as pertinent today, just with a changed target group. What happened in Brixton suggests that violent conflict between police and Travellers is likely in the future unless things change. The police called for more proactive methods to be undertaken but the clear message from the community was that they 'had had enough'. Taking the first step to bridge that gap to overcome the relationship of enemies and strangers was vital. I sensed frustration that although action was so urgently needed no one knew what to do to overcome the barriers.

Policing by consent and policing through dialogue with the communities had not so much broken down – it had never started. That was astonishing for 21st British policing.

A start can be made by dispelling the entrenched idea among the police that all Travellers are criminals. Such blanket labelling alienated the entire Traveller population. These issues could be resolved through dialogue but this would necessitate a leap of faith, abandonment of longheld assumptions and working *with* the communities.

The voices of Gypsies and Travellers in my research express cries for help. They cry out for action now to prevent future generations inheriting a desperate situation. Travellers have taken the first step, by asking for help. A Gypsy said emotionally 'I'm not here for me, I'm here for my grandchildren'. This may be a unique opportunity to make lasting change for services to Travellers. Travellers have shown their willingness – can the police respond?

The media and racist images

Training alone is not enough to tackle racism. But at the core of the problem lies improved training and strong leadership that is committed to justice. Gypsies and Travellers told the focus groups that the images that fuel the racism they face affect not just the police but the whole of society. Justice workers and Travellers alike recognised that overcoming racism entailed far more than what police training might achieve and far more than the singular efforts of the police could offer.

The origin of the powerful negative images in the media was identified. The police officers and Travellers returned continually to the media's representations of Gypsies and Travellers. 'The media give poor and negative publicity nationally about Travellers' said one Gypsy. Another pointed out how annoyed they were over the distortions of the media. They linked this distortion with the issues of identity and invisibility of Travellers and their lack of status, as discussed earlier.

In media representation we find one of the causes of Travellers' reputation. Gypsies described the stereotypical images – even caricatures – of the 'romantic Gypsy' or 'violent or criminal Gypsy' portrayed by the media. Travellers recounted how the images fuel perceptions about 'real Gypsies' which are in fact extreme stereotypes. The serious consequence of this is that Gypsies often struggle to find acceptance because of their apparent non-compliance with a popular media stereotype.

It seems there are real Gypsies and the Gypsies of the media. The popular images fed to the public by the media is hugely damaging to the communities. Gypsies already have enough problems with identity and hierarchy and particularly with the legal confusion and establishing rights within Race Relations legislation. Add to this the impact of the media 'playing games and peddling lies', as one Traveller put it, defeating efforts to overcome prejudice against them.

Seemingly supportive bystanders are generally unhelpful – indeed: 'sometimes well meaning people can fuel stereotypes by talking about the 'real Gypsies." Misleading representations in the media and literature become the simple 'reality' for many people in society who have never met a Gypsy or Traveller. In his analysis of epistemological power Foucault (2000) identifies the formation and preservation of identities and hierarchies as mechanisms of control. That negative images of Gypsies have prevailed for decades suggests a deliberate attempt at repression.

Travellers shared their frustration at apparently failing the stereotype test – somehow not living up to the images manufactured by the media.

> I have gone into schools and spoken to kids and the way I look and am does not fit their stereotype of what a Gypsy is.

They were angry about how the written representations of them are regarded as authentic even when they were written by people who had never met a Traveller. They knew about stories for children about Gypsies stealing children, written by popular authors like Enid Blyton. Stories can influence children in their formative years and such myths can become embedded. A Traveller blamed the fact that the literature is written about Travellers rather than by them, and said:

> It cannot just be read in books, if people are to realise that Gypsies don't have two heads you have to see them in the room. You need to talk to us, not just read the rubbish people write about us.

In the absence of authentic reference, stereotypes become the basis of popular information. Justice workers and Travellers resented the representation of an Irish Traveller, Mickey, in the film *Snatch* (2002) as a bare knuckle champion. The focus groups discussed the need for positive role models in the media. Whilst it was clearly important to get more positive representation, Travellers themselves need to establish their own image and identity: 'Gypsies need to be in a position to decide who are their role models, that's not for gorgers to decide'. Travellers need to assert themselves and tell their own story. As the Gypsy Council (2005) stated: 'Gypsy history is a history written by *gorgers*'.

Summary

■ Racism towards Travellers is common and overt

■ Police and Travellers view themselves as enemies yet strangers

■ Travellers appear to be at the bottom of a hierarchy of diversity

■ The media is fuelling negative images that many people believe accurately reflects Travellers

■ New generations of Travellers are angry about their treatment and representation

■ Too much has been written – inaccurately – about Travellers, and too little by Travellers themselves. Travellers need to assert their voice

■ Working together is the only way to move beyond a 'them and us' situation

5

The limitations of training

Much emphasis has been placed on diversity training in the police service (Rowe and Garland, 2003) but is it really what matters? This chapter makes it clear that training is not the sole answer to racism. This is such a vital message that I have devoted a chapter to trying to persuade future strategists to locate leadership at the centre of long term change. Diversity training in the police can be a self feeding matter, in a world of its own with little focus on skills and outcomes. The preoccupation with training too often takes the place of workplace application.

Throughout my research respondents kept telling me how they felt neither able nor permitted to question diversity training. Without a balance of common sense and democratic debate training becomes merely cosmetic. And even with much focus on racism all the training initiatives seem to have left the view towards Travellers unchanged.

We saw in Chapter 2 the depth of the stigma and anti-gypsyism (Hancock, 2002) that exists in the police service. Trainers who challenged this powerful anti-gypsyism risked becoming seriously isolated from their students. My research shows that it is still permissible to hold bigoted views towards Gypsies and Travellers. Overt racism may possibly have been redirected towards groups about whom it is more socially acceptable to be prejudiced. Some diversity training might actually equip racists if it fails to address the overt prejudice towards Travellers.

Some justice workers thought that diversity training is about covering backs: 'you've been told so it's now your problem'. This illustrates the alienation and cynicism some diversity training generates and shows that force-feeding race relations is counter productive. Diversity trainers who were involved in the research expressed their own frustration, asking: 'what can we achieve in one day's diversity training?' I see this frustration as positive, indicating their desire to genuinely make a difference. I hope this chapter can channel that positive motivation into more effective methods by examining ways of developing training for diversity.

Current methods of diversity training

My research revealed that much training is flawed in its implementation and methodology and, more fundamentally, because of its strategic approach. Practitioners expressed some strong views on what works in diversity training but they were stunted by the lack of dialogue among the practitioners so they could share and develop their practice. Practitioners also discussed the role of the community in training, and how the training environment could best optimise that contribution.

At the centre of the discussions about methodology was the trainer, whom they saw as a symbolic individual at the centre of diversity issues. This placed excessive responsibility on the shoulders of trainers. One of them argued that they were made to be the conscience of the organisation:

> There's a huge fudge in the police service, passing the buck up. Trainers should lead. The trainer's got a huge responsibility. If people don't want to be on the field they should be a spectator, if they don't want it, leave.

However worthy the trainers' motives have been, they have been misplaced because the workplace is were leadership on relationships with communities is needed. The idea of trainers as change agents for the service began in the late 1980s at the Turvey Centre for police training. Implementation of the vision of trainers becoming agents of change was not universal. Trainers felt unsupported on their treadmill of classroom delivery. Pizani Williams (1994) and Power (2004) both document the stress felt by trainers involved in diversity training, particularly concerning Traveller issues. I would add that the notion of trainers being agents of change is inevitably hampered by the classroom domain. Further, the focus on the trainer and the classroom – in that order – is part of the problem. The focus should be on the learners and the transference of learning into workplace outcomes.

A further problem for trainers is that they are cut off from systems of wider professional collaboration or education which inform policing learning and development. Trainers who did debate methodologies revealed strong idiosyncratic styles and showed little interest in extending their method or changing their style. I sensed a rather adversarial attitude amongst trainers which suggested that practice was unlikely to develop innovatively but would rather stagnate, become defensive and remain polarised.

How to do diversity training

The trainers spoke about the role of the diversity trainer in effectively engaging with students and about the role of the community in training. They discussed the best methods for diversity training and described three popular approaches.

Hearts and minds

The 'hearts and minds' approach is intended to appeal to students' better nature, feelings and ethical awareness, while also informing them about law and policy requirements, with perhaps some quantitative statistics to reinforce points. You might call it a carrot and stick technique.

Some trainers used more of the 'heart' or explorative approach, others more of the 'head' or instructive or legislative approach. These approaches are characterised by the view is that training should explore student views and address prejudice by working in an educative and self-reflective process supported by facilitation.

Exploration method: Why do you feel the way you do?

Some trainers found didactic techniques of little use and preferred to explore motivation – why people held prejudices. This approach was characterised by an educative and counselling process of exploration rather than merely signalling to halt certain behaviour. In the words of one trainer:

> There's no point in just saying 'you are wrong', you need to talk it through and find out what their experiences are and where they are coming from.

The exploratory style also took account of the environment:

> It's a good starting point to be able to let prejudices out. Training needs to be done in a safe environment where people do not feel attacked.

Trainers believed in the importance of the explorative and educative approach and did not wish to stifle discussion by challenging the negative views expressed as this would probably just drive them underground.

> I'm concerned about simply frightening people into stopping expressing their prejudices because this stifles debate and makes it more difficult to challenge. I admit I hold some prejudiced views about Travellers. I know people with other prejudiced views but with Travellers no-one sees a need to hold them in.

71

However, these trainers were aware that race and diversity training had the reputation of being difficult. They reported that much diversity training was perceived by operational staff as something on the periphery of police culture – 'pink and fluffy on a Friday afternoon', as one put it. It followed that training was not integrated into or widely supported in the workplace so was both physically and symbolically apart.

Instructive method: Don't do it, because...
An alternative to exploring prejudice, supported by Ellis (1962), is to challenge, as advocated by Wolpe (1958). The need to challenge behaviour was constantly raised in the focus groups, for instance: 'I think the first step is just to challenge generalised racist comments' and, even more decisively: 'I think you just challenge full stop!'

The discussion of challenge exposed two considerations. Some trainers said that whilst they agreed that challenging was the correct approach, it was not happening in relation to Gypsies and Travellers, including in their own practice. They felt ill-equipped: 'I think that not all trainers, perhaps most, would not feel confident to challenge or know when and what to challenge.' Does this mean that challenge would be the right training approach if it were done effectively?

The other consideration regarding the notion of challenge was the immense opportunity to do it. As one delegate pointed out: 'In training no stereotypes against gays and black people or other groups come out but prejudice against Gypsies still comes out.' Another argued that when overt prejudice was displayed it should be met with a formal challenge: 'We should be recording it as a racist incident and with an action plan about what we're doing about it.' But this approach also seems to require taking on managerial responsibility for acceptability and unacceptability in student behaviour. On one level this is realistic since police personnel in training are subject to all the normal professional requirements concerning behaviour but, practically, it places the trainer's facilitation role in awkward juxtaposition with trainer acting as manager.

A compromise is to be supportive of engaging with emotional understanding but to achieve a balanced training style by challenging cognition: 'We should be trying to change emotional views but also challenging things that appear factual.'

Can I say that? Safe learning environments

There was much debate about safe learning environments. Some argued: 'there is no such thing as a safe learning environment', others that 'trainers should not be enticing students to be inappropriate'. If the training methodology encouraged delegates to expose their prejudices the trainer could be seen as acting as *agent provocateur* in any disclosure of a criminal or disciplinary offence. Encouraging disclosure was one matter, knowing what to do with it when it came out was another. Concern about the need for safe learning environments was to one trainer 'the death knoll of any discussion'. Tomova (1999) notes that exploring emotive issues is psychologically risky and suggests caution unless trainers are well qualified and experienced.

But the need to establish openness remained vital to many trainers:

> You have to do the straight talking, let the anger out, we all have prejudices, put political correctness to one side.

Yet even the safe learning environment seemed selective – you could say certain things about some groups but not others:

> Going into training classes, I get lots of questions and comments. Such as – no Gypsies pay tax, all Gypsies rape the system, rip off old ladies, all tell lies, and see themselves as superior. I do challenge but when you have two people in a class feeding off each other standing up against the trainer at the front others won't stand up – would you say the things you say about Travellers about black people? No because they would be frightened I might report them.

Challenge could be risky for the trainer. There was a choice over whether to intervene or not. If you challenged negative discussions about Travellers, the risk of having your challenge rejected was higher. HMIC (2003) and more recently the CRE (2005) assert that trainers need to be supported in any challenges they make or they can lose their credibility. The Association of Police Authorities (2004) published advice that community representatives should not challenge students. However, my research revealed that they often did. In fact:

> The difficult issues are dealt with not by the police trainer but by the community trainer.

Sixty five per cent of trainers admit they feel ill equipped to deal with the prejudice towards Travellers (Coxhead, 2003) so it is likely that much goes unchallenged. Rejecting a trainer's intervention or challenge was not always direct 'If you pick the wrong time or subject the class can just freeze you out'. So is the choice between a challenge on grounds of principle or the tactical maintenance of functional group dynamics? Trainers were concerned that challenging comments would too often silence certain individuals, stopping the symptom but not the motivation. Was keeping the group talking no matter what the best option? This trainer thought so:

> You need to get people to open up so you can work with their views. It's not about being tidy it's about working with the mess.

The role of the communities

As well as methodology there was much debate about the role of community contributors. This revealed a tension over who was central: the police trainers or the community? Because with the majority of police trainers having difficulty coping with challenging racism about Gypsies and Travellers (Coxhead, 2003), they felt out of their depth. Trainers felt they lacked experience and understanding about Travellers and called for 'background information'.

> If someone said all black people are drug dealers someone would challenge it or point to positive role models in the black community but with Travellers it's harder to do that because I don't know of them.

And:

> The trainer doesn't have the positive experiences with Gypsies and Travellers to be able to challenge the racism when it comes out.

So did trainers think that interventions were better coming direct from the community, or from the trainer passing on the messages?

> I liked the story about the person who was not allowed to dump rubbish. Only problem is that it was third hand. I think we want first hand experiences at a training level rather than anecdotes...

> I don't think we have to have first hand accounts, it's just a matter of giving the information so that people can look at it from another point of view. It's about seed sowing and that's what anecdotes can do.

The knowledge required by the trainer affects the methodological issues. It is a valid point that the trainer cannot know everything but so is the fact that you cannot get every part of every community involved in all training. It was agreed that the best approach for community interface style training would be to locate the community at the centre of the event while the trainer facilitated so as to maximise opportunities for learning. This way there are no tensions about dominance, rather the synergy of complementary yet distinct roles.

However, community representatives should not be portrayed as victims:

> It shouldn't be bringing community members in to make people feel sorry for them. It's about people seeing the responsibility of the in-group, the power, not about feeling sorry for people.

The role of communities in police training and the danger of their simply being seen as victims has been noted by HMIC (2003) and the APA (2004). Recent guidance from the APA highlights the need for clear roles and agreements to help protect community contributors from inappropriate use in training events. From the trainers' accounts, it seems that 'too often trainers from communities have been humiliated'.

The key opportunity provided by involving the community is the interaction between them and the police service (Oakley, 1999; Korhonen, 2004). Community interface helps break down misunderstandings and addresses the demonisation of Travellers exposed by the police delegates.

This chapter seeks to clarify what the role of training is and is not. The generic points established by my research can ensure the future focus on diversity training is enhanced appropriately.

Firstly, any training undertaken must be helping to enable improved workplace performance:

> We have to measure success on service delivery, if there is not change for the community then it has not counted, it's not worked.

Secondly, this means evaluation must target outcomes not training inputs – they need to be real:

> It shouldn't be simply about saying the right things, it's about what you do. Race and diversity must be monitored as part of a performance indicator as essential practice.

Third, getting the community involved in training, whilst beneficial, should not be confused with the greater need to get the police working in the community. A community interface in training but never in the workplace extends the divide between training and workplace cultures, so that community engagement is not presented as core activity.

Once relationships are established, developing longer term community contact could support strategies such as those outlined by Rachman and Hodgson (1980). They found such contact helped break down negative perception and this parallels the approach taken in the *Pride not Prejudice* conferences which effectively 'brought people together' (Coxhead, 2004).

Fourth, although I am so critical of training, I have revealed some of the ways that it can be improved. Many of the specialist possibilities are signposted in this book, for example the specific application of meta-cognition. Training specialists will have to await further publications.

Finally, any improvement of professional practice will need to drive forward the message about why change was so essential. Any notion of training being responsible for how the police handle race and diversity is wrong and the lack of leadership on these matters identified by HMIC (2003) is strongly re-inforced by my research. So whilst there are ways in which training practice can be improved there are much wider lessons to be learned for core perfor-mance and the leaders who drive it. Given that the problems here are decades old, the message is clear: make progress together with the community in applied workplace outcomes or nothing will change.

Summary

- Training alone cannot create cultural change – the classroom is not the main arena in which to affect change

- Changing training methodologies can only result in doing the wrong thing better

- A focus on training in itself will achieve little

- Trainers do perform a type of leadership role, but this should not be mis-taken for workplace leadership, where the real changes can occur

- Strong and ethical workplace leadership is key to cultural change

- The involvement of the community in police training is to be welcomed but the greater goal is positive operational interaction with Travellers

6
The Way Forward

Are Gypsies and Travellers the last bastion of racism? There is no doubt that prejudice towards Gypsies and Travellers is a very real problem. Yet the overt nature of the prejudice offers an opportunity to explore and understand the aetiology behind the symptoms. The evidence of anti-racism and diversity training in the UK, Europe and North America, suggests that the patterns of bigotry share certain commonalities. The stories of oppression over time and place, of stigma and labelling are substantial enough to recognise that anthropologically, targets of bigotry may vary but they represent a common phenomenon. The common link is not the targeted group, but the bigot.

The solution is not to change the target but to change the bigot. The overt nature of prejudice towards Travellers gives us insight to tackle the bigot. This will benefit Travellers and every group that is subject to prejudice and discrimination. Despite decades of effort, there are still pockets of overt racism so the attempts made so far have been inadequate or a total failure. A new approach is needed to eradicate the behaviours of racism rather than allow bigotry, like some disease, to mutate and attack new targets.

The *Last Bastion of Racism* can be overcome only by focusing on the bigot and their behaviour, allowing no room for bigotry to shift its focus. So much work has been dominated by the background of the target group, as if to reinforce the notion that this is their problem, even though the constant feature of bigotry across the world is the bigot.

Some identified solutions were drawn from the research process. The practice and community insights described earlier have informed my ideas, particularly the need to go beyond training into a strategy for cultural change. Examples are important since they are specific, apply theory and ensure you see what I mean! This last chapter sets out some examples of how to apply the findings of the research so as to improve practice and challenge racism and bigotry. They indicate how long term cultural change can be driven through behaviour.

Listen

> Listen to excluded groups.
>
> Show people they are being heard and give them some of the power.
>
> Get people together in carefully constructed scenarios.

Hearing communities involves both the process and the conveyed content. Just telling someone and being heard can be therapeutic when this has never happened before. Set up a meeting of community members and your professional colleagues for the purpose of dialogue but more importantly for listening. For advice on the science of effective listening see Bentley (1994).

Facilitating listening between the groups can be complicated but listening is vital if in-groups and out-groups are to reach mutual understanding (Johnson, *et al*, 1991; Robson, 1993). I found that focus groups worked well. Plan it all well in advance. Choose a neutral meeting place which is undisturbed and free of interruption, and provide refreshments. Ensure that community representatives who are working on a voluntary basis receive appropriate recompense. Communities shouldn't be out of pocket for trying to help improve services to them. Invite ten to fifteen people and explain the purpose of the meeting beforehand. Spend time building trust during the introductions.

Allocate up to three hours and enable people to network afterwards. If you are hosting make your role clear. I found it best to not participate in the discussions as this freed me to keep an eye on things, and listen more attentively. You may need an independent note taker who records the key points made, and does so in a transparent way. The host needs to explain why notes are being taken so that people are comfortable about important points being noted. A relaxed atmosphere is essential if you want people to speak openly.

The research showed that a good way of bringing in-groups and out-groups together is to get them problem solving together. The problem statement should depersonalise differences so they are discussed as issues and not personality clashes. It is astonishing how much can be generated from getting mixed groups to work together on a common cause. Whilst the meeting is focused on what is discussed, the host can observe how the group dynamics of the process are working. I found the process of getting together usually has more impact than what is actually said. If you are bringing together groups who do not normally mix in positive ways, do not underestimate the importance of giving them a positive agenda.

Confer

Conferences are big business but they often fail to allow people to confer or discuss anything fully. But conferences that focus on community voice, networking and interaction do much to overcome barriers.

Use conferences as they were originally envisaged rather than what they have become (Coxhead, 2005). At most modern conferences one person stands at the front and talks at the rest of the people, who are usually sat in rows (Laurillard, 1993). Is this conferring?

An alternative, proved effective in my research, is to build on the approaches for suggested focus group, enlarging numbers to 200 in a suitable venue. Create a steering group comprised of all key stakeholders, so that from the start and throughout planning the communities have a voice. Have few formal speakers, and allocate plenty of time for networking and lunch – often the most productive time! Invite people to set up stalls and exhibitions and use recorded or live music to create an atmosphere of a celebration. This approach worked well with Travellers, who remarked that they did not normally bother with conferences as they were usually *about* them rather than *for* them. They themselves did their networking at fairs.

The research brought people together and showed them that utilising problem solving approaches gave them a common focus. A synergy of in-group and out-group agendas facilitated bonding, breaking down the adversarial views that ferment in isolation.

Three levels of interaction and consultation

A's view of B	**Remote**
A's view of B and B's view of A	**Adversarial**
A and B's joint discussion and mutual understanding	**Conjoint**

Youth and the future

> The youth agenda focuses on the future. Positive intervention and diversion by means of mentoring is a practical way of influencing behaviour. The focus on *Every Child Matters* (Children Act 2004) gives a common platform for all agencies, ensuring that positive wellbeing drives everyone's agenda.

Activities directed at youth are a wise investment. Apply principles of involvement to empower their voices. Issues facing Traveller youth have similarities with those faced by young people from other communities. They are too often excluded from decision making or volunteering their views.

Practitioners can use the framework of *Every Child Matters* (ECM, 2004), particularly the two pillars of 'making a positive contribution' and 'staying safe' as the desired outcomes for Traveller youth. Although young Travellers may have disproportionate risks of lacking safe homes because of the pressures of moving and the dearth of sites, the ECM agenda should certainly apply to Travellers. Specifically, justice professionals can work with Traveller Education support services in supporting families.

The ultimate way of influencing the future is to work with young people – but firstly we need to respect them. Unresolved issues within communities have built up frustration and anger. So practitioners need to find ways of working to a positive agenda whilst acknowledging their anger. Developing a cycle of positive action can acknowledge the injustices of the past and yet still be positive.

Thanks to ECM there is an established – and mandated – multi-agency work stream for young people. So there are identified professionals in other agencies who can work with you on agreed common outcomes. There are also existing funding streams you can tap into: both ECM and the national citizenship curriculum.

Getting people together when they are young is an ideal way of helping people grow together. Techniques used by the Black Police Association (BPA) in their Natural Born Leader programmes promote life coaching, overcoming self limiting barriers, using mentoring from positive role models and breaking free from exclusion and deprivation. Such positive activities and programmes should be made accessible to young Travellers.

Involving young Travellers in Youth Parliaments, for example, encourages their involvement in political decision making. There is already one Roma Gypsy MEP – Livia Jaroka. The glass ceiling for Travellers should be broken in every profession, just as for other groups.

Behaviourism as an intervention strategy

Focusing on what 'good' looks like is far more effective than rhetorical discussions.

My research findings reveal that people often believe they have reached consensus on a discussion point only to find difference when they move on to applying it. Effective approaches achieve behavioural change, clarify common understanding and build awareness.

One model is Vote Now. It uses a powerful film based case study – a snapshot of behaviour that illustrates workplace activity. Using a common assessment framework which lists behavioural outcomes (such as National Occupational Standards), the participants are asked to assess in real time the behaviour as performance. The discussion which follows explores judgement making, presumption, appearances, interpretation and identifies what good performance actually looks like.

Such an approach can be useful in offender intervention, for example, where views may differ about good behaviour is. Moving the agenda from rhetoric to focus on applied behaviour clarifies both the values and techniques of effective application.

The research findings stress the importance of driving cultural level change through individual behaviour.

Traditional model of change

Assumptions	Perceptions	Conclusions	Feelings	Behaviour

(APCFB psychological model: Darden Graduate Business School Foundation, Virginia)

Suggested model of change (Outperforming Prejudice)

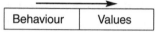

Behaviour	Values

National Occupational Standards

Sector Skills Councils have developed NOS

(National Occupational Standards) which list the appropriate behaviours for workplace performance.

National Standards provide a common framework for professionals to work according to measured behaviours and outcomes. NOS are developed by working with practitioners in each field to establish standard practice and this can be used to measure performance. If a common agreed set of standards is established which pays attention to fairness and justice, the standards can be a tool to drive cultural change.

However, reducing what can be highly complex behaviours and subtleties to a list can be problematic. Standards might be simplistic or too easy to achieve. Note that Standards are a minimum level, and the focus remains on outcomes. Standards do not replace management, leadership or motivation – this is still the job of the manager. But they do provide a clear set of performance behaviours for professionals to use to assess and improve their performance.

Performance Coaching

Performance coaching mainstreams the sanctions and rewards of behaviour into the culture of the workplace and is a catalyst for long term change.

Outperforming Prejudice and Inside Out both advocate local ownership of issues. The skills of trainers become the skills of the manager. The leader has to lead by example. Every manager is a leader, and every leader is a performance coach.

Key to performance coaching is the ability for leaders to review the judgements that are made. Judgements that are based on outcomes and use objective measures are about both the person being coached and the coach. A flexible approach in coaching to outcomes ensures that individuals are respected and empowered. Ultimately, good coaching is about empowering self coaching.

Practical ways of coaching entail observing and debriefing, or using simulated situations focusing on behaviours. The research found that good debriefing is about empowering the ability to self-debrief, consequently that integrity and ethics must be based on personal responsibility. Team building offers opportunities for bringing diverse groups together in activity and achievement focused outcomes (Star, Williams and Struffer, 1958; Hewstone, 2002). There are practical ways of applying sports coaching to support positive team activities to overcome bigotry (Cox, 2000). The research themes reinforce the value of a person-centered focus on behaviour (Rogers, 1951)*.

Socratic Facilitation

Socrates was famous for not answering questions but keeping the ownership of the issue with the student to ensure they engaged with it. Doing this avoids setting up a parent/child relationship. Overcoming bigotry necessitates taking personal responsibility for one's behaviour.

Socratic facilitation might appear to be a training technique but it is essentially a coaching strategy. It is similar to working in adult to adult mode using Transactional Analysis (Berne, 1964) with a focus on equality and democratisation. There is no hierarchical font of all knowledge so those involved have to take ownership of knowledge and skills. As the saying goes:

Give a man a fish and he will eat for a day.
Teach him how to fish and he can eat for life.

People need to find their own answers to problems. National standards of behaviours and outcomes provide a map to orientate by, but people own their own behaviour and have to understand this.

Socratic dialogue is characterised by consensual group decision making. Based on the philosophical stance of Socrates, a consensual resolution is sought to a problem by funnelling open questions into a 'symphony not a solo' (APPA, 2006). Neo-Socratic dialogue (Saran and Neisser, 2004) tends to focus on systematic questioning based on concrete experiences in order to develop one's thinking.

Socratic facilitation can be used as a coaching technique because it fosters and develops people's ownership of their own behaviour. It is a way of working with groups of people that ensures everyone is heard and respected. Facilitation is a good approach for implementing ethical values and avoiding oppression or bias (Zeni, 1998). The research used this approach successfully and certain principles can be identified that enhance the success of group based activities, particularly where community groups are stakeholders:

Do

- keep the groups small to help keep everyone on task

- invite stakeholders from both the in-group and out-group

- run several sessions with different delegates to ensure you establish common patterns or themes

- discourage any segregation: in-groups and out-groups need to come together

- help identify the key questions and encourage everyone to contribute

- try to establish the points of agreement and divergence before the groups leave.

Don't

- use meetings with stakeholders as an opportunity to rubber stamp decisions that have already been taken

- impose your views on a group

- focus on people's personalities: do focus on issues

Normalising justice

Many Travellers feel that in practice justice is not available to them. Yet processes of justice do exist in the agencies and the courts. What is new is the inclusion of Travellers within the processes of justice.

Time after time the experience of Travellers was revealed as being extraordinary or abnormal – they were over policed and under protected. A virtuous cycle could be prompted by working with Travellers as communities rather than treating them as a problem. Giving people a stake in the processes of justice grants them a place as victims and witnesses and not just as offenders. It means that there could be a straightforward policing service on a day to day basis that included Travellers in a consensual relationship. When they experience rounded services they will see for themselves that provision has become fair. The research suggests that all it needs is to make services more like those normally provided to other ethnic groups. Normalising policing would apply existing skills in community policing to ensure consistent policing services for Travellers.

A gap analysis is a useful tool of diagnosis.

Positive recruitment to improve representation of social group	Are you including Travellers?
Monitoring service provision for legal compliance and quality	Do you have a forum to monitor service that includes Travellers?
Working *with* people	Do you mutually problem solve issues with Travellers or talk 'about them' between yourselves?
Standardised policies	Wherever you cite 'Traveller' would you be comfortable with substituting 'black'
Part of the problem or part of the solution?	Out-groups remain so by the reinforcing of negative stereotypes. Do you challenge this and promote the positive characteristics of Travellers?

Equitable resources = balance and trust	Look where you put your efforts – do you spend £1 on positive resources for every £1 on punitive resources?
You get out what you put in: How do you spend your time?	How much time is spent in confrontation with Travellers compared to dialogue?
Show me the evidence!	Note down when you have genuinely consulted or liaised with Travellers over service provision.

Wherever you find gaps in normal provision it is obvious what needs to be done. Applying the skills habitually used with other communities: listening, spending time, seeking mutual understanding, ensuring messages are actioned and ensuring that justice is seen to be done, and so on. Experience in the justice system of working positively with communities is widespread, be it with black communities, Chinese communities, gay communities, mining communities, Jewish communities. So the test is easy, look for abnormality and replace it with normality. This in itself helps overcome one of the breeding grounds of bigotry – the negative reinforcement of difference by creating caveats which seem to justify certain treatments for certain people.

Travellers who contributed to my research discussed how sincerely gratified they were when they were treated with genuine respect and transparent fairness by justice workers. Travellers were keen to point out that justice must be based on what people do, not who they are. Travellers need to see balanced and normalised justice demonstrated.

These principles can support the immediate and long term goals to overcome bigotry. The strategies of bringing in-groups and out-groups to work together generates change at a cultural level. Consistent reinforcement of the behaviourist approach is recommended, to ensure people work together as people rather than being fixed on stereotypes.

If we already had a scientifically verifiable method of eradicating bigotry we would not require books such as this. The unique contribution of my research lies in the insights from people who have experienced racism rather than from academic bystanders. Some of my suggestions and approaches seem straightforward to the point of obviousness but much can be learned by listening to the voices that speak to us through the research.

The book keeps the wider context always in view. Prejudice towards Gypsies and Travellers is not a local matter, nor is it just within the UK: it is a global problem. Overcoming bigotry is far more than a task for police training; it is a challenge for society. The Police Service seeks to reflect the society it serves, and this is why the challenges identified here need to be owned by society in general.

The Last Bastion of Racism? Well, the problem never was with the groups being victimised. The enemy is not the out-group but the social patterns or working conditions that relegate certain people to an out-group. When people stop being seen as people and start becoming 'them' you have bigotry. To attack the last bastion requires working alongside people rather than opposing them. It means always understanding them, listening to them, focusing on outcomes. The fundamental strategy for tackling the last bastion is to engender responsibility in everyone concerned so that they see others as individuals and start changing their behaviour accordingly.

Endnote

*Further references for the interested reader can be found in Bond (2002) and Bennet-Levy *et al*, (2004). Some prefer the general approach of cognitive behavioural psychology (CBP) as opposed to psychodynamic or gestalt approaches, because there is less emphasis on trying to pin down unconscious motivation, and more attention is given to the action of observable behaviour. In simple terms, CBP acts as a form of reinforcement, using motivational levers of reward and punishment. For example, stopping at a mandated traffic junction is done without much thought. Psychodynamic psychotherapy explores why we behave in particular ways: why we might, or might not, stop at a traffic junction. Although the cognitive behavioural approach is less sophisticated than some areas of psychological practice, it offers a pragmatic and immediate technique for performance coaches.

Bibliography

ACPO (2004) web site < http://www.acpo.police.uk/ >

Acton, T. (1998) *Authenticity, Expertise, Scholarship and Politics: Conflicting Goals in Romani Studies.* University of Greenwich

Acton, T. and Dalphinis, M. (2000) *Language, Blacks and Gypsies: languages without a written tradition and their role in education.* London: Whiting and Birch

Alderson, J.C. (2004) *Principled policing: Protecting the public with integrity.* London: Waterside Press

All London Teachers Against Racism and Fascism (1984) *Challenging Racism.* London: ALTARF

Allport, G. (1959) *The Nature of Prejudice* (1979 reprint). London: Wesley

APA (Association of Police Authorities) (2004) *Involving communities in police learning and development: a guide.* APA

Augustine, J. (2004) 'Joint Initiative with the Canadian Association of Chiefs of Police', *First Nationals Chief of Police Association*, 26-08-03

Babchuk, W. (1997) 'Glaser or Strauss?' Grounded Theory and Adult Education Paper, Mid West Research-to Practice Conference, Michigan Sate University October 15-17, 1997

Bancroft, A. (1999) 'Gypsies to the Camps! Exclusion and Marginalisation of Roma in the Czech Republic' *Sociological Review* Online, Vol. 4, No.3, (Paras.4.1)

BBC (2003) *The Secret Policeman*, documentary featuring Mark Daly screened 20 October 2003

Bedford, S. (1999) *Porraimos: The Devouring.* Northampton County Council

Belson, W.A. (1986) *Validity in Survey Research.* London: Gower

Bentley, T. (1994) *Facilitation: Providing Opportunities for Learning.* Maidenhead: McGraw-Hill

Berne, E. (1964) *Games People Play.* Harmondsworth: Penguin

Bernstein, B. (1974) *Class, Codes and Control*, Vol. 2. London: Routledge

Bethrong, D.J. (1963) *The Southern Cheyennes.* Norman: University of Oklahoma Press

Bigler, R. S. (1999), 'The use of multicultural curricula and materials to counter racism in children', *Journal of Social Issues* Winter 1999

Birmingham Evening Mail 29.06.93: 1

Black Britain Online Magazine (2004) (03-11-04) 'Antiracism trainers harassed by police' <http://www.blackbritain.co.uk>

Bond, F. (ed.) (2002) *Handbook of Brief Cognitive Behavioural Therapy.* Mahwah NJ: Erlbaum

Brown, J.M. and Campbell, E.A. (2004) *Stress and Policing: Sources and Strategies.* Chichester: John Wiley

Burrel, G., and Morgan, G. (1979) *Sociological Paradigms and Organisational Analysis.* London: Heinemann

Burtonwood, N. (2002) 'Holocaust Memorial Day in schools – context, process and content: a review of research into Holocaust education', *Educational Research*, 44 (1) pp. 69-82.

Cacciapuoti, G. (1998) *Focus Groups: Strengths and Weaknesses.* Rome: Giulio Cacciapuoti

Carr, W., and Kemmis, S. (1986) *Becoming Critical: Educational Knowledge and Action Research.* Deakin University Press

Central Advisory Council for Education (1975) *Children and their Primary Schools* (The Plowden Report). London: HMSO

Centrex (2004) *Race and Diversity Trainers Course* < http://www.centrex.police.uk/ >

Chan, J. (1997) *Changing Police Culture: Policing in a Multicultural Society.* Cambridge University

Cohen, S. (1971) *Images of Deviance.* Harmondsworth: Penguin

Cohen, S. (2002) *Folk Devils and Moral Panics.* London: Routledge

Commission for Racial Equality (2004) *A Formal Investigation of the Police Service in England and Wales, An interim Report*, June 2004 CRE

Commission for Racial Equality (2004) *Gypsies and Travellers: A strategy for the CRE, 2004 -7.* CRE

Commission for Racial Equality (2005) *Final Report of the formal investigation of the Police Service in England and Wales.* CRE

Cook, T. (1998) 'The importance of mess in action research' in *Educational Action Research*, Vol 6, No. 1

Covey, S.R. (1999) *Principle Centered Leadership.* New York: Simon and Schuster

Cox, R.H. (1998) *Sports Psychology: Concepts and Applications.* Duboque, Iowa: W.C. Brown

Coxhead, J. (2003) Questionnaire from police national diversity trainers' network (unpublished)

Coxhead, J.D. (2003a) 'Rethinking tackling prejudice' unpublished paper give at Faculty of Education, University of Cambridge, 20.06.03

Coxhead, J.D. (2004) 'Theory and Practice: the thought of coming together', *Race Equality Teaching* 22(3)

Coxhead, J.D. (2005) 'Have you tried talking to one?', *Race Equality Teaching* 23(2)

Coxhead, J. (2005a) Focus Group data (2004-2005) unpublished

Danflous, R. (2007) *Policing in relation to Roma, Gypsy and Traveller Communities.* OSCE – ODIHR Western European Regional workshop, European Dialogue, London

Darden Foundation (1986) 'Why People Behave the Way They Do', *School Case UVA-OB-183* Fig. 5, p. 16, Charlottesville, Virginia: Darden Graduate Business School Foundation

Da Vinci (2002) <www.leonardodavinci.fi/tools/tiedofuschjeistus_en10-2004.pdf>

Davies, A and Thomas, R. (2004) Dixon of Dock Green Got Shot!: Policing Identity Work and Cop Culture Cardiff Business School, unpublished

Dawson, R. (2000) *Crime and Prejudice: Traditional Travellers.* Oxford: Blackwell

Dawson, R. (2006) *Stop and Search: A National Survey.* Oxford: Blackwell

Debo, A. (1995) *A History of the Indians of the United States.* University of Oklahoma Press

Department of Education and Science (1985) *Education for All: the report of the committee of enquiry into the education of children from ethnic minority groups* (Swann Report), HMSO

Dunning, E., Murphy, P. and Williams, J. (1988) *The Roots of Football Hooliganism.* Routledge

Eck, J. and Spelman, W. (1988) 'Problem solving – problem orientated policing' *Newport News,* US Dept of Justice, National Institute of Justice, Washington.

European Vocational Training (2002) Dissemination. *European Vocational Training News,* Winter, 2002

Ellis, A. (1962) *Reason and Emotion in Psychotherapy.* New York: Lyle Stuart.

Essed, M. (1991) *Understanding everyday racism: An interdisciplinary Theory.* Newbury: Sage

Findlay, M., and Zvekic, U. (eds.) (1993) *Alternative Policing Styles: Cross Cultural Perspectives.* Boston: Kluwer Law and Taxation Publishers

Foreman, G. (1932) *Indian Removal.* University of Oklahoma Press

Foucault, M. (2000) *Power.* New York: The New Press

Fox, M. (1993) *Psychological Perspectives in Education.* London: Cassell

Friedman, I. R. (1990) *The other victims: first person stories of non Jews persecuted by the Nazis.* Houghton Miffin Co., Boston

Garfinkel, H. (1968) *Studies in Ethnomethodology.* London: Prentice Hall

Gibbs, A. (1997) 'Focus Groups'. *Social Research Update* Issue 19

Glaser, B. G. (1992) *Basics of Grounded Theory Analysis: Emergence versus Forcing.* New York: Sociology Press

Glaser, B.G. and Strauss A.L. (1967) *The Discovery of Grounded Theory.* Chicago

Goss, J.D. and Leinbach, T.R. (1996) Focus groups as alternative research practice, *Area* 28(2): 115-23

Gundara, J., Jones, C., Kimberley, K (eds.) (1986) *Racism, Diversity and Education.* Sevenoaks: Hodder and Stoughten

Gypsy Council (2005) 'The Road Ahead' Conference, 22.04.05, Blackpool

Halsey, A. H. (1972) *Educational Priority Volume 1: EPA problems and policies.* HMSO.

Hancock, I. F. (1996) *Land of Pain: five centuries of Gypsy slavery and persecution.* World Romani Union, Budapest

Hancock, I. F., (2002) *We are the Romani People.* University of Hertfordshire Press

Handy, C. (1993) *Understanding Organisations.* Harmondsworth: Penguin

Harrop, A. (1983) *Behaviour Modification in the Classroom.* Sevenoaks: Hodder and Stoughton

Hesse, B. (1993) 'Racism and spacism in Britain' in *Tackling Racial Attacks* Francis, P. and Matthews, R. eds. Leicester: Centre for the Study of Public Order, University of Leicester

Hewstone, M. (2002) Intergroup bias and Social Prejudice, *Annual Review of Psychology.* New York: Gale Group

Hill, J. and Kerber, A. (1967) *Models, Methods and Analytical Procedures in Education Research.* Wayne State University

HMIC (2003) *Diversity Matters.* HMSO

Holdaway, S. (1996) *The Racialisation of British Policing.* London: Macmillan

Holdaway, S. (2003) Police Race Relations in England and Wales: Theory, Policy and Practice. *Police and Society,* Issue No. 7 2003

Home Office (2004) *A Strategy for improving performance in race and diversity 2004-2009.* Home Office, http://www.homeoffice.gov.uk

Home Office (2004) *Initial Police Learning and Development Programme* (IPLDP). Home Office <http://www.homeoffice.gov.uk>

Home Office (2005a) *Neighbourhood Policing.* Home Office <http://www.homeoffice.gov.uk>

Home Office (2005b) *Moving Forward: How the Gypsy and Traveller Communities can be more engaged to improve policing performance.* Home Office <http://www.homeoffice. gov.uk>

Hudack, G.M. and Kihn, P. (2001) *Labelling Pedagogy and Politics.* London: Routledge Falmer

Institute of Employment Studies (2003) *Training in Racism Awareness and Valuing Cultural Diversity.* Practice Report no. 23, Home Office

Ivatts, A.R. (1975) *Catch 22 Gypsies.* London: Advisory Committee for the Education of Romany and other Travellers

Ivatts, A.R. (2003) Roma/Gypsies in Europe Paper delivered at the UNESCO World Conference, Finland, June 2003

Jefferson, T. (1990) *The Case Against Paramilitary Policing.* Milton Keynes: Open University Press

Johnson, D.W. and Johnson, F.P. (1991) *Joining Together: Group Theory and Group Skills.* London: Prentice Hall

Jupp, V. (1989) *Methods of Criminological Research.* London: Routledge

Kenny, M. (1997) *The routes of resistance: Travellers and secondary level schooling.* Aldershot; Ashgate

Kenrick D. and Clark, C. (1999) *Moving on: the Gypsies and Travellers of Britain.* University of Hertfordshire Press

Kitzinger, J. (1994) The methodology of focus groups: the importance of interaction between participants. Sociology of Health and Illness vol. 16, no.1, 103-121

Korhonen, A.R. (2004) Exchanging experiences in police diversity training project study visit to London 22-27 January 2004, unpublished

Krueger, R., A. (1993) *Moderating Focus Groups.* London: Sage

Lather, P. (1991) *Getting smart: feminist research and pedagogy with the postmodern.* London: Routledge

Laurillard, D. (1993) *Rethinking University Teaching.* Routledge

Lowe, R. and Shaw, W. (1994) *Travellers – Voices of the New Age Nomads.* London: Enabler Publications

MacGreil, M. (1996) *Prejudice in Ireland Revisited.* Maynooth: St Patrick's College

BIBLIOGRAPHY

Macklin, R. (1999) Understanding Informed Consent, *Acta Oncologica*, 38 83-87

Macpherson, W. (1999) *The Stephen Lawrence Inquiry Report.* London: Stationery Office

Mandela, N. (2004) *Long Walk to Freedom.* New York: Abacus

Mandla Criteria see *Mandla v Dowell Lee* (1983) 2 AC 548 (HL)

Marsick, V., O'Neil, J. and Watkins, K. (2001) 'Action Learning' in Wadawski, J., and Church, A. (Eds.) *Handbook of Organizational Development.* CA: Josey-Bass

Mason, D. (1999) *Race and Ethnicity in Modern Britain.* Buckingham: Open University Press

McConville, M. *et al* (1991) *The Case For The Prosecution: police suspects and the construction of criminality.* Routledge.

McCormick, L. and James, M. (1983) *Curriculum Evaluation in Schools.* (2nd Ed.). London: Croom Helm

McNamee, M. and Bridges, D. (eds.) (2002) *Ethics and Educational Research.* Oxford: Blackwell

Meichenbaum, D. (1974) *Cognitive Behavior Modification.* California: General Learning Press

Melykuti,F. (2000) *Towards community policing: the police and ethnic minorities in Hungary.* University of Louisville

Meyer, W. (1979) Informational Value of Evaluative Behaviour: Influences of Social Reinforcement on Achievement, *Journal of Educational Psychology* 71(2) (1979): 259-268.

Morgan, D.L. (1993) *Successful focus groups: advancing the state of the art.* California: Sage

Morris, R. (2000a) Gypsies, Travellers and the Media: Press Regulation and racism in the UK, *Communications Law* Vol. 5, No. 6, 2000

Morris, R. (2000b) The Invisibility of Gypsies and other Travellers, *Journal of Social Welfare and Family Law,* January 2000

Morris, R. (2001) Gypsies and Travellers: New Policies, New Approaches, *Police Research and Management,* Vol. 5 No. 1 2001

Morris, R. and Clements, L. (1999) *Disability, social care, health and Travellers,* Traveller Law Research Unit, Cardiff Law School

Morris, R. and Clements, L. (1999a) *Gaining Ground: Law Reform for Gypsies and Travellers,* Traveller Law Research Unit, Cardiff Law School, University of Hertfordshire Press

Morris, W. (2005) *The Morris Inquiry.* London: Stationery Office

Niner, P. (2002) *The Provision and Condition of Local Authority Gypsy/Traveller Sites in England* ODPM. London: Stationery Office

Nuwer, H. (1999) *Wrongs of Passage: Fraternities, Sororities, hazing and binge drinking.* Indiana University Press

O'Brien, M. et al (2000) *Institutional Racism and the Police: Fact or Fiction?* Institute for the Study of Civil Society, Cromwell

O'Nions H. (1995) The Marginalisation of Gypsies, *Journal of Current Legal Issues,* 1995

Oakley, R. (1994) *Police Training concerning migrants and ethnic relations.* Council of Europe

Oakley, R. (1999) Report of Turvey Workshop 4-6 March 1999 < www.errc.org/cikk.php >

Office of the Deputy Prime Minister (2004) *Definition of the term 'gypsies and travellers' for the purpose of the Housing Act 2004.* London, Stationery Office

Okely, J. (1983) The Traveller-Gypsies, Cambridge University Press

O'Hanlon, C. and Holmes, P. (2004) *The Education of Gypsy and Traveller Children: towards inclusion and educational achievement.* Stoke on Trent: Trentham

Oppenheim, A.N. (1992) *Questionnaire Design, Interviewing and Attitude Measurement.* California: Pinter

Osler, A. and Starkey, H. (2004) *Changing Citizenship.* Buckingham: Open University Press

Paul, A. M. (1998) Where Bias Begins: the truth about stereotypes, *Psychology Today* May/ June: 52ff

Pettigrew, T.F. (1958) Personality and sociocultural factors in intergroup attitudes: a cross sectional comparison, *Journal of Conflict Resolution*, 2:29-42

Phillips, T. (2004) Speech, 18th October 2004, CRE Press Release Ref. 896

Pizani Williams, L. (1994) *Gypsies and Travellers in the Criminal Justice System: the Forgotten Minority?* Cambridge University Press

Police Review (2005) *Police Review*, 25.03.05, Jane's Publishing Group

Power, C. (2004) *Room to Roam: England's Irish Travellers.* Manchester: Community Fund

Powney, J. and Watts, M. (1987) *Interviewing in Educational Research.* London: Routledge

Pride not Prejudice (2005) <www.pridenotprejudice.org.uk>

Rachman, S. and Hodgson, R.J. (1980) *Obsessions and compulsions.* London: Prentice Hall

Reich, B. and Adcock C. (1986) *Values, Attitudes and Behaviour Change.* London: Methuen

Reiner, R. (2000) *The Politics of the Police.* Oxford: Oxford University Press

Rowe, M. and Garland, J. (2003) 'Have You Been Diversified Yet? Developments in Police Community and Race Relations Training in England and Wales' *Policing and Society.* Vol. 13. No.4, Dec. 2003

Rowe, M. (2004) *Policing, race and racism.* Willan Publishing

Robson, M. (1993) *Problem Solving in-groups.* Aldershot: Gower

Rogers, C. R. (1951) *Client-Centered Counselling.* Boston: Houghton-Mifflin.

Rosenthal, R. and Jacobson, L. (1968) *Pygmalion in the Classroom: Teacher expectations and pupils' intellectual development.* New York: Rinehart and Winston

Rosenthal, R. and Rosnow, R.L. (1991) *Essentials of Behavioural Research.* New York: McGraw-Hill

Saran, R. and Neisser, B. (eds.) (2004) *Enquiring Minds: Socratic Dialogue in Education.* Stoke on Trent: Trentham

Scarman Report (1981) *The Brixton Disorders.* London: HMSO

Schein, E. (2004) *Organisational Culture and Leadership.* California: Jossey-Bass

Schmidt, R.A. and Wrisberg, C.A. (2000) *Motor Learning and Performance: A problem solving based learning approach.* Champaign IL: Human Kinetics

Scriven, M. (1986) Evaluation as a paradigm for educational research, *New Directions in Educational Evaluation*, Lewes: Falmer

Singh, G. (1993) *Equality and Education.* Derby: Albrighton Publications

Ska Films (2002) *Snatch.* Sony Films

Skolnick, J.H. (1994) *Justice Without Trial.* New York: Macmillan

Smirchich, L. (1983) 'Concepts of culture in organisational analysis' *Adm Sci Q* 1983; 28, 328-358

Star, S.A., Williams, R.M. and Struffer, S.A. (1958) Negro infantry platoons in white companies in *Readings in Social Psychology.* New York: Holt Rinehart and Winston

Strauss, A.L. and Corbin, J. (1994) Grounded Theory Methodology: An Overview, in N.K. Denzin and T.S. Lincoln (eds.) *Handbook of Qualitative Research.* Thousand Oaks: Sage

Stringer, E. T. (1999) *Action Research: A handbook for practitioners.* Thousand Oaks: Sage

Tomova, I. (1999) Training of teachers and students for military schools in understanding ad tolerance towards ethnic and religious differences and work with Roma, Inter ethnic initiative, Bulgaria, unpublished.

Townshend, C. (1994) *Making the Peace: Public Order and Public Security in Modern Britain.* Oxford: Oxford University Press

United Nations Educational, Scientific and Cultural Organisation (1977) *Ethnicity and the Media.* UNESCO, Paris

Van Cleemput, P. (2004) *The Health Status of Gypsies and Travellers in England.* University of Sheffield

Van de Ven, A.H. (1974) The effectiveness of nominal, Delphi and interacting group decision making processes, *Academy of Management Journal* 17 (4), 605-21.

Velasquez, M. (2004) *Screening Diversity Trainers,* Diversity Training Group, USA

Walker, S. (1984) *Learning Theory and Behaviour Modification.* London: Methuen

Wiesenthal, S. (1986) Tragedy of the Gypsies, *Bulletin of Information* 26, Vienna: Dokumentationszentrum des Bundes Judische verfolgter des Naziregimes

Wiesenthal, S. (1989) *Justice not Vengeance.* London: Weidenfield and Nicolson

Winter, R. (1998) Finding a Voice – Thinking with Others: a conception of action research, *Educational Action Research,* Vol. 6, No. 1

Wolfendale, S., Bryans, T., Fox, M., Labram, A. and Sigston, A. (eds.) (1991) *The Profession and Practice of Educational Psychology.* London: Cassell

Wolpe, J. (1958) *Psychotherapy by reciprocal inhibition.* Stanford University Press

Yoong, P. and Pauleen, D. (2004) Generating and analysing data for applied research: a grounded action learning approach, *Information Research,* Vol. 9, No.4

Zeni, J. (1998) A guide to Ethical Issues and Action Research, *Educational Action Research,* Vol. 6, No. 1

Zsaru magazine, (2005) *Romak es rendorok,* January 5 2005, page14, *Observer* Budapest

Index

ACPO 36
Acton, T. 60
Acton, T. and Dalphinis, M. 29
Alderson, J.C. 52
All London Teachers Against Racism and Facism 35, 40
Allport, G. 28
Association of Police Authorities 36, 75
assumption cycles 44
Augustine, J. 32, 34
authoritarian personalities 44, 59

Babchuk, W. 5
Bancroft, A. 38
BBC 39
Bedford, S. 25
behaviourism 3, 81
Belson, W.A. 3
Bentley, T. 78
Berne, E. 25
Bernstein, B. 4
Bethrong, D.J. 27
Bigler, R.S. 44
Birmingham Evening Mail 29
Black Britain Online Magazine 35, 38
Bond, F. 87
Brown, J.M. and Campbell, E.A. 52

Bulgaria 40
Burrel, G. and Morgan, G. 4
Burtonwood, N. 43

Cacciapuoti, G. 3
Centrex 6, 11
Chan, J. 34, 35, 38
citizenship 81
Cohen, S. 48
Commission for Racial Equality 26, 28, 31, 59, 61, 73
Conference 75, 79
Cook, T 5
Covey, S.R. 8, 9, 12, 14
Coxhead, J.D. 38, 57, 73, 79
Danflous, R. 54
Davies, A. and Thomas, R. 47
Dawson, R. 53, 62
Debo, A. 27
Delaney *see* Johnny Delaney
Department of Education and Science 6
Diversity Matters, 36-38
Dunning, E., Murphy, P. and J. Williams, J. 33

Eck, J. and Spelman, W. 3
Ellis, A. 42, 44, 72
Essed, M. 29, 32
ethics 47, 83

evictions 50-51
exploding skills 20

facilitation 71-72, 83-84
Findlay, M. and Zvekic, U. 51
Firle 64
Foreman, G. 27
Foucault, M. 31, 67
Fox, M. 43
Friedman, I.R. 25, 44

Garfinkel, H. 4
Gibbs, A. 4
Glaser, B.G. 4-5
Glaser, B.G. and Strauss A.L. 5
Goss, J.D. and Leinbach, T.R. 3
Gundara, J., Jones, C and Kimberely, K. 40
Gypsy Council 68

Halsey, A.H. 5
Hancock, I.F. 26, 28, 30, 60, 69
Harrop, A. 43
Hawthorne effect in research 3
hazing and initiation rites 52
Hesse, B. 6
Hewstone, M. 38-39, 44, 59, 61, 83
Hill, J. and Kerber, A. 3

97